If you are fortunate enough, you meet a person in life who changes you for the better. Laura Joan Katen is one of those people. I've had the privilege of getting to know Laura through her work at CBS. Her dynamic style and ability to personally connect with people in small settings, in large settings, and in written form helps her effectively offer practical communications strategies that bring immediate results. She's been a difference-maker in my life and can be in yours as well. That's why I strongly recommend you add The Communication Habit *to your "must-read" list—to help you and those you wish to inspire around you.*

—MARLENE BAEZ
Vice President, Human Resources
CBS Television Studios

Laura is a master communicator. Her dynamic approach to classroom facilitation and coaching addresses an array of diverse interpersonal needs for all learners. The result? Improved communication outputs and better business culture. I highly recommend The Communication Habit *for your own personal benefit and for the benefit of those you collaborate with in the workplace.*

—STEPHEN HUNT
Professional Development Lead
Talent Development, Human Resources
Mercedes-Benz USA

In the first seven seconds of meeting Laura, one understands that she is highly intelligent, focused, and impressive. A leader in the field of professional development, Laura possesses the rare ability to listen deeply, provide sound advice, and offer her uncanny understanding of leaders—what makes them tick, what they want, and how you can use that knowledge to build bridges and boost your career. If you're looking for effective methods to communicate your value and navigate workplace challenges, I unequivocally recommend The Communication Habit.

—CHARITY ELDER
former Head of Video and Podcasts
Yahoo News

Laura is a true expert in communication and professional presence. Many people can talk the talk, but Laura walks the walk. She personifies professionalism and elegance in a consistent and authentic manner. She is a true pleasure to work/partner with and always brings her "A game." As a professional in the Learning & Development field, providing my organization with the best of the best is always my top priority, and Laura fits the bill perfectly. It has been my sincere pleasure to work with her for more than five years, and I'm confident that we will continue to partner for many years to come.

—KELLY RESTAGNO
Director of Learning & Development and Training
Luxottica Wholesale North America

The Communication Habit *is a must-read for anyone working in finance or business. Laura shares invaluable insights and actionable techniques for communicating effectively—from how to "speak someone else's language" to how to be a more impactful listener. It's a win-win all around. As a woman on Wall Street, I found the chapter on Articulating Your Value and its emphasis on tactful self-promotion quite significant. Readers will be empowered to highlight wins to management, increase their visibility, and build their brand.*

—ALLISON KATEN
Managing Director and Head of Institutional
Equity Sales—North America, HSBC

In a knowledge-based economy, possessing excellent communication and interpersonal skills is a distinguishing feature for anyone in a managerial or leadership capacity. No one understands this better than Laura Joan Katen, whose speaking engagements on the topics of presentation, executive presence, and business etiquette have long been a highlight of our MBA program. Laura's content expertise is matched by her unique ability to connect with her audience and quickly convert undermining habits and apprehension into poise and confidence. The Communication Habit *reveals the key markers of successful executives and entrepreneurs and in doing so makes the case for why this book is a must-read for everyone.*

—Timothy Landers
Assistant Dean and MBA Director
Anisfield School of Business
Ramapo College of New Jersey

Laura has a special ability to convey a message in a way that will influence people to act. Her delivery is powerful, precise, and on point. She is passionate about helping people break through their limiting beliefs. Laura is a great communicator because she is authentic, and that is fully reflected in her work.

—Mzia Bekuraidze
Retail Director Elie Saab USA,
Global Haute Couture Designer

Laura Joan Katen offers a unique perspective on communication that transforms everyday conversations into opportunities for connection and representation. Her skill is guiding learners to understand the transformative value of language to represent themselves in authentic ways. Laura's expertise as a communicator is evident in her dynamic and innovative facilitation techniques. She brings that creativity to her new book, The Communication Habit. *I strongly recommend this book from those just beginning their career to senior leaders.*

—Sharon Folkes
Director of Training and Development
New York City Department of Transportation

We have seven seconds to make an impression, and Laura's is that of a master communicator. I have been in learning and development for 30 plus years and have never come across a better expert in the field of communication than Laura Joan Katen. Whether she is delivering her message to an audience of 30 or 1,000, each participant leaves with a better understanding of his or her communication style and techniques to develop it. It's exciting to know that she is sharing that wealth of expertise with the world in her new book The Communication Habit. *I highly recommend it.*

—JULIANNA WIESSNER
Chief Learning Officer
New York City Government Agency

Laura's dynamic and engaging approach to speaking and coaching addresses the needs of all learners. She has an uncanny ability to make learning relevant and fun; her strategies resonate across generations and from novices to experienced professionals. Regardless of experience, we can all learn something new from Laura; see for yourself by reading The Communication Habit.

—MELINDA GERMAN
Associate Dean, Undergraduate Business Programs
Villanova University School of Business

Extraordinary knowledge and skill in the area of communication—that is what you get when you see Laura in action during one of her training sessions. Now Laura is sharing her expertise, which you can use immediately both professionally and personally. The Communication Habit *is a book that you will want to have at hand to help you navigate and negotiate communication strategies for success. Most of what we do involves good communication— let Laura guide you with her proven techniques.*

—SUSAN ZEIDMAN
former Vice President, Learning & Development
Clever Devices

THE
COMMUNICATION
HABIT

THE
COMMUNICATION
HABIT

STRATEGIES THAT SET YOU APART
AND LEAVE A LASTING IMPRESSION

LAURA JOAN KATEN

NEW YORK CHICAGO SAN FRANCISCO ATHENS LONDON MADRID MEXICO CITY
MILAN NEW DELHI SINGAPORE SYDNEY TORONTO

1 2 3 4 5 6 7 8 9   LCR   25 24 23 22 21 20

ISBN   978-1-260-45916-6
MHID   1-260-45916-0

e-ISBN   978-1-260-45917-3
e-MHID   1-260-45917-9

McGraw-Hill Education books are available at special quantity discounts to use as premiums and sales promotions or for use in corporate training programs. To contact a representative, please visit the Contact Us pages at www.mhprofessional.com.

To my inner circle.

To all of the people who have supported me and given me
the opportunity to do what I love every day.

To AMK, RNK, JAMK, GMK who always make sure
I bring my A game.

CONTENTS

THE JOURNEY BEGINS . . .   ix

CHAPTER ONE
FIRST IMPRESSIONS AND PERCEPTIONS   1

CHAPTER TWO
CREATING AN ACCURATE IMPRESSION   23

CHAPTER THREE
PROJECTING CONFIDENCE AND PRESENCE   71

CHAPTER FOUR
SPEAKING WITH INTENTION   89

CHAPTER FIVE
COMMUNICATING YOUR COMPETENCE   137

CHAPTER SIX
ESTABLISHING CREDIBILITY 197

CHAPTER SEVEN
RECOVERING, REBUILDING, AND REESTABLISHING 215

FINAL THOUGHTS 231

NOTES 235

INDEX 239

THE JOURNEY BEGINS . . .

This book is all about you. It's about helping you to recognize and reinforce your strengths and increase your awareness of what you could
be unconsciously doing to undermine your success—and the perception that you want others to have of you.

The information and strategies shared in this book stem from the
thousands of questions, concerns, and challenges that I've been asked
about, best practices shared, and the many important topics broached by
professionals across geography, industry, position, and gender. It's geared
toward the standards of professional business environments in the United
States. This information may very well be appropriate for application in
other countries and corporate cultures that have similar business standards and customs. If you work abroad or for an international company
based in the United States, it's also essential that you learn the specific
country's customs and courtesies as well as the particular workplace's
culture, expectations, and norms.

Throughout this journey, I will share important research and information, offer opportunities for coaching, and address how to navigate
some of the most common and awkward workplace situations. I encourage you to take a moment to think about the exercises and questions
posed in the "Coaching Corner" and how the information highlighted, or
the questions asked, impact you. It's in these moments, when you turn the

mirror inside and think about how the information shared relates to you, that self-discovery and growth happen.

Some of the challenges and concerns consistently shared with me include:

"How do I deal with 'difficult' people?"

"What can I do to be a better listener?"

"How can I effectively communicate with higher-ups?"

"How can I get myself heard in a meeting?"

"What can I do to build my confidence when communicating?"

"If I'm seen as unapproachable, how do I fix that?"

"How do I stop someone from hijacking the conversation without damaging the relationship?"

COACHING CORNER

What are some of the challenges that you face when it comes to effectively communicating or interacting with others?

Challenges

By being aware of the communication challenges that you face, you can start to think about which strategies highlighted in the pages of this book will help you to best address them.

You are officially on your way to setting yourself apart and making a lasting impression at work. Here's to learning the subtleties and secrets to achieving greater success!

THE
COMMUNICATION
HABIT

FIRST IMPRESSIONS AND PERCEPTIONS

We do not see things as they are, we see things as we are.
—ANAÏS NIN
French-American writer

The goal is for you to have the tools you need to make a positive first—and lasting—impression that's a true reflection of your strengths and core values—and, ultimately, be perceived by others the way you envision. This chapter highlights four key elements of making an impression—and the subtle nuances that contribute to the perceptions that others form of you. Knowing this information can help you to increase self-awareness, leverage your strengths, and focus on areas that may need more of your attention.

In order to increase self-awareness, it's important to look inward.

COACHING CORNER

How do you want to be perceived by others in your professional environment—and are you being perceived that way?

Using the table below, in the first column list three to five words that express how *you* would like to be perceived by others in your work environment.

In the second column, list three words that reflect how your manager perceives you. This can be based on performance evaluations, nonverbal clues, emails, and conversations you've had with your manager.

In the third column, list three words that describe how your direct reports perceive you. If you don't have direct reports, list words that describe how your colleagues perceive you. This can be based on nonverbal clues, emails, comments you've received—or a 360-Degree Assessment that gathers anonymous feedback from your direct reports, colleagues, and leaders.

Me	Manager	Direct Reports or Colleagues

Now take a moment to review your list of words side by side. Is how you *want* to be perceived aligned with how you're *being* perceived by others? If yes, wonderful; keep up the good work! You will learn to reinforce and strengthen that positive perception by the information included in this book. If no, don't worry. By picking up this book, you're already on your way to increased self-awareness, growth—and, ultimately, to being perceived the way you want.

If you had trouble coming up with the three words for how you want to be perceived by others, that's important to note. If you don't know *how* you want to be perceived, how can you make the choices that will help you to be perceived the way *you* want? In addition, if you had difficulty coming up with words for how your boss perceives you, it's important to find out. How can you be confident that you're being perceived the way you want by leadership, if you're not sure how leadership perceives you?

Perception happens instantly and, often, unconsciously. Knowing what you're being evaluated on can help you to make a positive first, and lasting, impression.

Seven seconds . . . or less!

Research shows that you have 7 to 30 *seconds*—and often *less than* 7 seconds—to make a first impression.[1] That's no time at all. How can we expect to impress anyone in seven seconds or less?

You *can*, and I'll share with you *how*.

FOUR CORE AREAS OF A FIRST IMPRESSION

For the last several years, I've traveled over 100 days a year giving keynote talks, leading workshops, and engaging with a wide range of professionals. I've had the opportunity to answer questions from individuals across geography, industry, position, rank, and gender—smart, skilled, and successful men and women. They are leaders at all levels: new hires, aspiring managers, employees who feel "stuck" and want to get promoted, those seeking to impress senior leadership, and others who wish to take their experience and knowledge to other organizations. Throughout all of my interactions and engagements, I've concluded that there are four core areas that people consistently use to evaluate one another.

1. Appearance

2. Communication

3. Interactions

4. Social Business Etiquette

Research shows that within the first few seconds of meeting you, people make certain significant determinations. These impressions are a result of both conscious and unconscious stimuli, including:[2]

- Education level

- Competence

- Level of sophistication

- Trustworthiness

- Economic status

Individuals can unconsciously undermine themselves in one or more of the four core areas—this is usually due to a lack of self-awareness. Could the same be true with you? Could you be undermining yourself?

The key is to be "in the know"—to have information that allows you to make deliberate decisions and create the perception of yourself that you envision.

The following sections highlight important aspects of the four core areas of a first impression.

Appearance

Appearance is the totality of what you're visually communicating. The parts include body language, attire, accessories, and grooming and hygiene.

COACHING CORNER

Take a moment to consider . . . What are you visually communicating at work?

Body Language

Body language is such an important topic in communicating the right message that I've dedicated all of Chapter 3 to it. Therefore, let's continue by taking a closer look at the other aspects of appearance and a few key strategies.

Attire

The standards, expectations, and guidelines around what constitutes acceptable and appropriate professional attire constantly shift with the world around us. They are impacted by several factors, including country code, company culture, comfort, trends, industry, position, and personal preference.

When considering what to wear, think about what you want to *visually communicate*. Choose attire based on the following five guidelines and ask yourself the accompanying questions:

1. **Fit: How does each piece fit?** Are you sacrificing fit for fashion? Improper sleeve-length, a blazer so snug that you're unable to button it when standing or move your arms with ease, or pants that are the wrong size or length can make you feel self-conscious and undermine a confident presence.

2. **Fabric: Is the fabric appropriate for both the season and the work environment?** Could the fabric be perceived as too casual, unprofessional, or outdated for the company culture or your role?

3. **Color: What characteristics do you want to communicate?** Colors can play a key role in how you're perceived. They can increase your visibility, reflect a confident presence, exude positivity, and distinguish you. They can also undermine your appearance by making you blend into the background and create misperceptions about your energy and personality.

   One of my favorite colors in the professional arena is navy blue. Studies show that navy blue implies intelligence and reflects approachability, confidence, trust, and professionalism.[3] It's also true that the best colors for you are the ones that make you feel comfortable, confident, and reflect your professional responsibilities, personality, and aspirations.

4. **Pattern: What is the purpose of the pattern?** Patterns can be a great way to add interest and a little pop of personality to any professional ensemble. Be careful, as busy patterns can be distracting and detract from your appearance—and your message.

   When it comes to adding a pop of color or pattern to an outfit, a great option is through accessories. A tie that pulls colors from the shirt and suit, a pashmina wrap, jewelry, or patterned socks, suspenders, and a silk scarf are effective ways to add a dimension of interest to your look and create a polished appearance that pops.

5. **Style: Does the style reinforce your personal brand?** Whatever your personal style, make sure that it's appropriate for your position, your industry, the current time period, and the company dress code. You also want it to contribute to your sense of confidence—when you feel confident about how you look, it impacts so many other aspects of what you project. While you certainly want your style to reflect your personality, ensure that you're also respecting company policies and the general work environment.

Paying attention to these details will help ensure that your attire is supporting the perception you want others to form of you. Here are a few more key strategies when it comes to your overall appearance:

- **Whom do you admire?** Observe those in your professional environment who are in the positions to which you aspire. What are they wearing? If they make a positive and polished impression, what specific attributes stand out?

- **Dress for the position you want (while taking into consideration the position you have).** Show that you're committed to your success and are confident, competent, and professional—all without overshadowing your boss or alienating yourself from those around you.

- **Ask your mentor or advocate for guidance.** A mentor is an invaluable resource for many professionals. He or she is someone who can guide you in the professional realm and be an impartial sounding board. A mentor can span gender, industry, and position—and give you unbiased, objective guidance and feedback. If you don't have a mentor, I highly recommend you consider finding one (see Quick Tip).

The topic of appearance is often brought up by participants. Their questions usually revolve around finding *the balance* between being true to themselves, and their personal preferences, and making sure they're

---

QUICK TIP

Finding a Mentor—a Trusted Advisor

Here are a few tips to get you started if you don't have a mentor:

- Think about a successful man or woman within, or outside of, your professional arena who is truly invested in helping you achieve your goals.

- Share with this individual what led you to ask him or her—and how this person's background, journey to success, or current role is well aligned with your individual aspirations.

- Connect for a brief introductory chat—and then plan phone calls or meetings on a more regular basis. While your conversations or catch-up meetings will be according to the mentor's availability, it's essential to note that the mentee drives the relationship. You're the one reaping the benefits of this professional's success, time, insights, and guidance; be proactive in connecting, show appreciation, and always prepare in advance for your meeting or call.

also seen as fitting into their work environment and not undermining themselves. Sometimes getting an outside perspective can help to reinforce that you made the right decision, which allows you to "wear" your choice with confidence.

Being aware of the subtle details of your appearance could mean all the difference to the impression others form of you. A deliberate detail that can help your outfit take center stage is your accessories.

Accessories

Accessories are a wonderful way to add another aspect to your look, complement your outfit, and enhance your overall image. The *right* accessories can add the finishing touches to any ensemble. In addition to the accessories themselves, the number and quality of accessories worn communicate a message.

Similar to your attire, you want to avoid choosing accessories that detract or distract. As a starting point or in a highly conservative work environment, consider limiting yourself to three accessories (in addition to any necessary items: glasses, wedding band or engagement ring, and watch). Then, based on the totality of your appearance, decide if something needs to be removed. In some industries, less is more—while others expect and respect a flashier statement. As famed fashion icon Coco Chanel once said, *"Before you leave the house, look in the mirror and take one thing off."*[4]

Two important points to note—pieces of your attire can count as accessories. If your outfit has very bold colors, distinct fabric, ornate stitching, or multiple patterns, these details may pop enough that additional accessories could look overwhelming—in this case go lighter on the accessories. Also, if wearing a statement piece—an accessory that is more substantive in size, bold in color, distinct in structure, instantly draws the eye to it, or is worn because it reflects a certain sentiment or makes a deliberate statement—a good guideline for staying professional without being distracting is to count it as two accessories.

Just as wearing too many or the wrong accessories might undermine a polished look and the image you're trying to project, not wearing any accessories could undermine your goal of establishing a notable visual presence and translate into the misperception of your being "less experienced."

Besides attire and accessories, the final core area of appearance is your grooming and hygiene.

Grooming and Hygiene

The nonverbal element of grooming and hygiene plays a core role in the perception someone forms of you—and is defined as how clean and neat you appear as well as the health and wellness of your body. The critical importance of this core area is further reflected in studies that show when it comes to appearance, the top factors for reflecting executive presence are grooming and polish.

Your appearance is one of the primary ways that managers and colleagues assess your professional abilities—and potential. A polished appearance reflects intent, respect, and thoughtfulness. Studies also show that more often than not, it will also translate into how others perceive the quality of your work product.[5] Giving thought to your image, to your visual brand, will empower you to be perceived the way you want.

QUICK TIP

The Importance of Executive Presence

It's important to highlight executive presence when speaking about first impressions and perceptions, because the impression that many professionals want others to have of them is that they exude a notable presence.

Harvard Business Review defines executive presence as "Your ability to project mature self-confidence, a sense that you can take control of difficult, unpredictable situations; make tough decisions in a timely way and hold your own with other talented and strong-willed members of the executive team."[6] Many of these core characteristics are reflected indirectly in how people position themselves during those initial first few seconds of interaction.

Communication

Communication, or a lack thereof, can often be the source for your work-place successes and frustrations. Some of the key categories of communication that can help or hinder the perception that others form of you include:

- Nonverbal messaging

- Vocal delivery

- Words

- Listening

- Structure and organization of the message

- Written and e-communication

- Social media etiquette

Communication is such an invaluable skill, and reportedly one of the top three most widely sought-after skills by employers,[7] that in addition to being the second core area of a first impression it's also our core focus throughout the rest of this book.

Interactions

The ability to interact effectively, build rapport, and make others feel at ease around you is key to distinguishing yourself—and it's the third core area of a first impression.

The benefits and value of soft skills and of being someone who can easily interact with others, and has the know-how to navigate common and awkward workplace situations with diplomacy, tact, and credibility, are often the subject of daily blogs, articles, and research.[8] The conversations surrounding interpersonal skills, and the vital importance of how individuals conduct themselves, seem to have been widely known for decades—with a study being traced back to 1918. Harvard University, Stanford Research Institute, and the Carnegie Foundation examined if there is a connection between how you conduct yourself and the level of professional success you achieve. The answer was yes. "Technical skills accounted for less than 15 percent of one's value in obtaining, keeping, or advancing in a job. More than 85 percent of job success is based on personal conduct and the ability to put others at ease."[9]

How you conduct yourself and interact with others matters. Knowing how to navigate common and awkward conversations and interactions with consideration, confidence, and resolution has become increasingly more important for professional mobility and merit. Your image and interactions with others can often be a distinguishing factor when competence is the norm.

There are many different aspects of interactions that are important to master—we all start in the same place: with a greeting. And for many, that is a handshake.

The Art of Handshaking

The gesture of handshaking can instantaneously help to build rapport and reflect competence, respect, trustworthiness, and confidence. If not done well, it can also communicate discomfort or disinterest.

When you're in a culture or business environment that expects and respects handshaking, there are subtle nuances that can help make your handshake most *memorable* and support the positive perception that you want others to form of you.

Here are a few subtle nuances to mastering the handshake. Unless there are extenuating circumstances, a standard handshake is initiated with the right hand. The fleshy part between your index finger and thumb is called the web. Your web must fully connect to someone else's web to give a proper handshake. Curl your fingers around the other person's hand and pump two or three times, then release. It's one fluid motion stemming from the elbow—not the wrist or shoulder. The two words you want to remember are *firm* and *brief*. If you're too delicate, you could be misperceived as nervous, weak or give the impression that you're lacking confidence—and even trustworthiness. If you're overly strong or have an overzealous grip, you may be remembered as being a bone crusher or misperceived as trying too hard to build rapport or mask discomfort. As with most things, handshaking requires a balance *and* awareness. You don't want to be remembered for the wrong reasons.

When shaking hands or being introduced to someone, in most situations—if and when possible, you'll want to stand. Standing is another way you can show respect for people, and it puts you in a position to easily make eye contact with the other person.

Handshaking Faux Pas

The Finger Shake

When your webs don't connect, the result is a "finger shake." This doesn't reflect the same positive impression or characteristics as a firm, brief handshake.

If you're the receiver of the "finger shake," one option is to quickly wiggle your hand into the web-to-web position. You can also use humor to defuse any tension as you smile and say, "Let me try that again." Either option may seem awkward at first—both are effective ways to honor that you'd like to give a firm, brief handshake and truly connect with this person.

The Glove Shake

This shake is defined by the action of using two hands. An individual extends a standard right-handed shake and then covers the recipient's hand with his or her left hand. This handshake is often seen as a compliment because it's the initiator's way of expressing warmth, in a professional arena, toward the receiver. The intention behind the "glove shake" is to build connection quickly, utilize it when a kiss or hug may not be comfortable or appropriate, and honor the recipient with more warmth than a standard shake.

It's also a shake that can easily be perceived as infringing on someone's personal space. A good guideline for personal space in the United States is approximately two arm's lengths, which is the distance of a handshake. Once you touch the other person's hand, elbow, back, or shoulder while shaking hands, you have invaded that two arms' length space and might unknowingly make the receiver uncomfortable. Make your determination based on your rapport with the recipient and *his or her* comfort.

The Pat Shake

Patting the receiver's hand with your left hand while giving a standard right-handed shake can reflect affection or be seen as a condescending gesture. Avoid giving a "pat shake" since it can be perceived as patronizing.

The Power-Play Shake

You may have noticed this handshake with some political figures or senior leadership in your organization. An individual gives a standard right-handed shake and then turns the receiver's hand over so that his or her palm is facing up. With this handshake, the initiator is in the more dominant role and has placed the receiver in a less powerful position. It's also important to mention that this gesture may not be intentional. Some initiators habitually bend their wrists inward while shaking hands, giving the appearance, without having the intention, of a "power-play shake."

If you're the receiver of the "power-play shake," my guidance is to readjust your handshake to the proper technique and put yourself back on an even playing field with the initiator. If you're the receiver of other faux pas shakes, make a mental note for future interactions with those individuals—and lead the shake next time.

The key is to avoid using any of the handshakes highlighted unless you are consciously making the strategic choice to do so.

Alternative Greetings

With roughly 7.7 billion people in the world and 329 million individuals in the United States, there's a diversity of cultures, religions, capabilities, and comforts to consider. When you're in a culture, business environment, or among individuals who expect and respect handshaking, this gesture can instantaneously help to build rapport and reflect competence, trustworthiness, and confidence. Conversely, if you're in a business culture that is less ceremonious, you see someone on a more regular basis, or you interact with individuals who instinctually offer an embrace or for religious or other reasons prefer not to touch, a standard handshake may be too formal or improper. In these environments, shaking hands could reflect disinterest and create discomfort or distance. This is when alternative greetings such as smiling, nodding, giving a verbal greeting, jumping into small talk, or reciprocating a culturally customary hug, wave, or kiss on the cheek may work better.

Whether gesturing "hi," handshaking, or hugging your "hello," the key to effective interactions is making others feel respected, welcome, and at ease around you. The overarching element is to set a positive tone from the start by acknowledging the other person—how you do that is up to you.

QUICK TIP

Protecting Your Personal Space

If you're on the receiving end of a hug—and you don't like to be touched or have your personal space invaded—there is a subtle strategy to honor your comfort without embarrassing the initiator. Smile, verbally greet this individual while extending your handshake *sooner* than you normally would to greet others, and lock your elbow. Shaking with a straight arm is a tiny tweak that will help to protect your personal space by preventing the person from getting too close. Smiling and verbally greeting this individual will be the focus— without it they may be more apt to notice the shift. All most people care about is that they are greeted and that they feel welcome around you—how you choose to do that depends on the person and the context of the exchange.

COACHING CORNER

How do you honor your personal comfort while still making others feel welcome around you?

Throughout this book, we will continue to address key situations and answer frequently asked questions that will help you to progress your interpersonal success.

Social Business Etiquette

The last of the core areas of a first impression is social business etiquette, which consists of your manners and behaviors, engaging in common courtesies, and your ability to effectively navigate food, drink, and conversation in a business setting. Some places requiring skilled interactions and social business etiquette include:

- Industry networking functions and work events

- Holiday parties and cocktail receptions

- Business meetings over a meal

- After-work happy hours

- Client engagements and events

The ability to exhibit confidence, competence, and manners in a work-related social setting is another layer that contributes to other people's perceptions of you.

COACHING CORNER

Have you ever been put off by the way someone ate?

Is there a habit that you have around food or drink that could potentially undermine you in the eyes of others?

Here are a few guidelines for social business situations.

- **Strategy #1: Know your goal.** Social business events always have a business-related purpose. Consider the purpose ahead of the event itself so that you fulfill that expectation—such as getting face time with a key client, building rapport with your team, interacting with senior management, or meeting others in your industry.

These events require a similar level of professionalism and self-awareness that you would exhibit in the office.

- **Strategy #2: Have food *or* a beverage.** Demonstrate your interest in attending the event by having a plate of appetizers or a beverage in your hand. Not eating or drinking anything may give the impression that you're removed from the event with no interest in being there. It's essential to choose one or the other—it's about building rapport, not about the food.

  If you opt for an alcoholic beverage, remember that it's still a work-related function—so stay professional. A number of elements, including how much you ate that day, can quickly shift an innocent action into an apology.

The key is to honor what's comfortable for you,
in regard to eating and drinking, while still making
others feel that you're participating.

- **Strategy #3: Engage in effective small talk.** When thinking about how to start the conversation, find a commonality—such as the reason that brought you to the event, knowing the host or one of the same guests, or that you both have similar roles for different companies. Then, to keep the conversation progressing, share something about yourself. You have to give to get. Once that happens, ask your conversation partner a noninvasive open-ended question and then use the information received to ask a follow-up question to keep the momentum going.

Pyramid of Small Talk

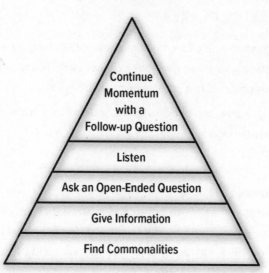

Continue
Momentum
with a
Follow-up Question

Listen

Ask an Open-Ended Question

Give Information

Find Commonalities

If you get stuck, when it comes to making small talk, because you're afraid asking questions could seem invasive, asking the right questions may be the differentiating factor. Think about asking questions that allow the recipient to answer in any number of ways, and don't require too personal an answer, and reflect you're listening and interested, such as:

How did you get involved in _____?

When did you realize you were interested in _____?

Tell me more about _____

What changes have you seen with _____?

According to research published in the *Journal of Personality and Social Psychology*, people who ask follow-up questions are better liked by their conversation partners.[10]

Stay mindful of these social business etiquette strategies the next time you head to an event, and you will be able to focus more on quality conversations and building rapport and worry less about potential pitfalls.

COACHING CORNER

Reflecting on the four core areas and various techniques of a first impression, what are three conscious decisions you make to have others form a positive perception of you?

What is an action or behavior that you now realize may be undermining you?

Perceptions are subjective. Even when you do everything possible to present yourself with polish and professionalism, people will still form their own conclusions. The essential difference is that by having this information on your radar, continuously acquiring knowledge, and increasing your self-awareness, you will be better equipped to make deliberate decisions that lead you to being perceived the way you want.

YOUR QUESTIONS ANSWERED

The strategies shared in this book stem from the thousands of questions, concerns, and challenges that I've been asked about by professionals across geography, industry, position, rank, and gender.

At the end of each chapter in this book, you will find some of the most common Q&As that relate to the chapter. These may be helpful in your journey to further distinguish yourself and make a long-lasting positive impression.

1. *"Should a man wait for a woman to extend her hand first?"*

In many cultures that expect and respect handshaking and in the current US business climate of gender equality, it's acceptable for either a man or a woman to extend a hand first and initiate a handshake—unless you're meeting Her Majesty, the Queen of England. If that is the case, wait for the Queen to extend her hand and refrain from holding it tightly or pumping it.[11]

When meeting individuals from other cultures, it's incredibly important to understand the acceptable protocol. If you can't tell if a handshake would be appropriate, then extend your hand. If the gesture is not reciprocated for any reason, be gracious by simply pulling back your hand, smiling, and greeting the person verbally.

2. *"I'm horrible at remembering names. Any tips?"*

Remembering someone's name demonstrates that you care, are a good listener, and it's a great way to build rapport. Some strategies for remembering names include:

- Repeat it on meeting—and then, sparingly, integrate it into the conversation.

- Ask (with a smile) the individual to repeat it.

- If you've met in the past and can't recall his/her name, start by stating your own—and politely ask the person to remind you of his/hers. (A friendly way to break the ice is by stating that you recall meeting in the past—or remember his/her face. The other person will feel a bit more important knowing you at least remembered meeting.)

- Ask the person to spell out his/her name when the name is hard to hear, difficult to pronounce, or if you're connecting virtually.

- Make a quick seating chart if you're in a meeting. List people's names, reflecting where they are currently seated in the room, while they go around and introduce themselves.

- Ask for a business card at the *beginning* of a conversation; this way you can glance at the card throughout the conversation.

- Invite someone to add their contact information to your phone.

- Use word association, such as: connecting someone's name to a key attribute or physical characteristic they possess or to a friend or celebrity with a similar name.

3. **"What if I don't care enough to make small talk?"**

Making small talk is a pivotal part of interpersonal success. You may not care about making chitchat or the person with whom you're speaking. It's still a key way to break the ice, build and sustain rapport, and help people to feel comfortable around you. Therefore, try looking at making small talk from a more personal angle—*investing in your own success.* Focus on what you do genuinely care about—you. If you can authentically care about making small talk because you know it will support your personal growth and professional development, and the perception others form of you, you may find making small talk easier—and even enjoyable.

4. **"I don't drink. I sometimes feel awkward when everyone is drinking around me. Is there something I can do?"**

Don't ever feel pressured to drink alcohol. If someone creates an uncomfortable situation for you, teases or questions you, simply respond, *"I'm enjoying my drink."* Or raise your glass and say, *"You should try this, it's delicious."*

Another option is to take the onus off of you by asking the bartender to make you a delicious house-special "mocktail"—the venue's signature cocktail with no alcohol. This way when questioned you can say, *"I asked the bartender to make me the house special—it's delicious."*

It's important that you believe it's okay not to drink alcohol and that your delivery reflects that confidence. Responding with ease and assurance will set the tone that you're fine with your decision, cannot be riled, and you may even indirectly give someone else "permission" not to feel pressured into drinking.

Depending on the sophistication of the event, you can also ask the bartender for your beverage in a wine glass. This may help you to feel more a part of the group.

My goal is to stay sharp, professional, and polished at work-related events. Therefore, I often opt for a nonalcoholic beverage. Most people don't care *what* you're drinking; all they really want to know is that you *are* participating. Having any beverage in hand will do that. Having a confident, friendly answer when asked will deter others from teasing or questioning you.

. . .

With this deeper understanding of key elements that contribute to a favorable first—and lasting—impression, think about how *you* want to be perceived—and know that your decisions and actions are critical for achieving that result. Now that we've laid a solid foundation for making a polished, professional, and confident first impression, in general, let's explore specifically how *you* can create an *accurate* impression of yourself.

CHAPTER TWO

CREATING AN ACCURATE IMPRESSION

Chains of habit are too light to be felt,
until they're too heavy to be broken.
—WARREN BUFFETT
American investor, Chairman and CEO
of Berkshire Hathaway

Other people's perceptions of you can considerably affect your level of success. They can impact the level of respect you receive, if you're given a voice at the table (or invited back to the table), your pay, and whether or not you get promoted. Creating an accurate impression of yourself is based on two things:

1. Knowing how *you* want to be perceived and leveraging your strengths

2. Understanding which of your habits may be undermining you—and being more aware of how those tendencies impact other people's perceptions of you

COACHING CORNER

Take a look at the following chart. For each row of words, put a check in the "Self" column if you see yourself that way—and/or a check in the "Others" column if you think others perceive you that way.

	Self	Others		Self	Others
Confident			Arrogant		
Responds			Reacts		
Commands			Demands		
Assertive			Aggressive		
Interjects			Interrupts		
Passionate			Emotional		
Listens			Hears		
Concise			Vague		
Refers			Reads		
Friendly			Friends		
Self-Promotes			Brags		

Both columns reflect powerful words. The words in the left column are predominantly positive attributes—versus the words in the right column, which are often associated with more negative connotations. Understanding the subtle differences between similar words will allow you to make deliberate decisions and to reflect actions that ensure you're being perceived the way you envision.

The key is to be aware of the subtle differences
between each pair of words.

Let's examine how quickly two opposing perceptions can be formed.

1. *CONFIDENT* VS. *ARROGANT*— DISMISSIVE DEMEANOR

Confidence is being comfortable in your own skin, believing in your abilities, feeling secure in who you are, and knowing the value that you bring. Arrogance can be defined with similar characteristics, with the main difference being the dismissive demeanor or attitude that accompanies this personality trait. It can create the perception that others' ideas, contributions, or time are not as valuable as one's own.

Here are some examples of these two types of people in action:

Confident: *"I hear you. My thought on that is . . ."*
Arrogant: *"As I said before, my thought on that is . . ."*

Confident: *"That must have been difficult for you."*
Arrogant: *"That's not as difficult as what I had to go through."*

Confident: *"Let's take a look at this from another perspective."*
Arrogant: *"You're wrong."*

COACHING CORNER

What are some behaviors that you've exhibited that could be misperceived as arrogant instead of confident?

As we look through the lens of potential misperceptions, another important distinction is the difference between the words *responds* and *reacts*.

2. *RESPONDS* VS. *REACTS*— LACK OF TIME

Time is the primary difference between someone who responds and someone who emotionally reacts. People who respond take a moment to think before they speak, email, or act. They maintain composure, are in control of their emotions, and can calmly navigate uncomfortable and awkward situations and conversations.

Think about an individual you know who is consistently calm and collected—even when there's a crisis. Research shows that this display of "gravitas" is a key characteristic admired by many and that those who reflect executive presence consistently exude it.[1]

Then there's the person who reacts by yelling at subordinates in front of people—or who is calm one minute and angry the next, forcing you to walk on eggshells.

COACHING CORNER

Do you consider yourself to be someone who thoughtfully responds—or reacts out of emotion?

Individuals who emotionally react allow their emotions to have control over them—and dictate their actions. These persons are often perceived as less rational, intimidating, or having poor judgment; as a result, they may be passed over for projects, pay raises, promotions—and more.

If you're someone who emotionally reacts, and you're looking to modify that behavior, it's important to understand the physiological reason behind it. The brain first receives new information through its reptilian and limbic lobes.[2] These are the parts of the brain that cause instinctual reactions and are considered to be your emotional center. As a result, a knee-jerk reaction may occur. In order to respond rather than react, the information you internalize needs time to be processed so that it reaches your rational-thinking neocortex brain. Time will help to shift the information from the emotional center to the logical center of the brain, thereby reducing the emotional reflex. Feeling (and reacting) *before* thinking can set a person back professionally—resulting in the need to recover, rebuild, and reestablish rapport—and one's reputation. Being aware of this physiological process is the first step in improving this behavior.

Following are some other techniques for responding versus emotionally reacting.

Make a "PACT" with Yourself:
Pause, Assess, Choose, and Take

P = Pause. Take a moment to pause and breathe. Depending on the severity and context of the situation, and the person with whom you're speaking, step back to gain some perspective. Instead of speaking right away, you can make a few mental, emotional, and physical adjustments:

- Excuse yourself from the situation.

- Walk to get a coffee while considering your options.

- Take a deep subtle breath to calm your inner monologue.

- Remind yourself to listen—and not say anything in the heat of the moment.

- Verbalize that you need a moment to process what was just said or done and that you would like to circle back with this person later in the day.

A = Assess. Take a moment to reflect on what happened and try to logically assess the situation. Is it serious? Did the person intend what he or she said? Could you have misinterpreted the tone of the email? You may want to gain some additional perspective by speaking with a mentor or confidant.

C = Choose. Choose your course of action. There are three primary options you can consider:

- *Respond.* After assessing the situation, you're clear and comfortable with how you would like to respond.

- *Wait.* After assessing the situation, you're not ready to respond, realizing there may be other aspects of the situation to consider.

- *Ask.* After assessing the situation, you're still unsure how to interpret the other person's intentions, words, or actions. In this case, ask questions for clarification.

T = Take. Now that you've chosen the way you want to respond, take action. Whether you decide to respond, wait, or ask for more information—do so respectfully and professionally. By practicing PACT, you will empower yourself to be in control of the situation and the perception that others form of you.

Of course, there may be extenuating circumstances when you need to emotionally react. No matter the situation, be mindful that it's the underlying *intention* that determines the perception that others form of you.

The key is to know which behaviors you want to define you.

Responding When Blindsided

In order to be perceived the way you want and not negatively labeled by others, it's essential to be able to respond in difficult situations. As former First Lady of the United States Michelle Obama has said, "When they go low, we go high."[3] It's in these tense moments, after being blindsided, or when unpleasant feelings are welling up, that you want to rise above.

Here are a few ways to respond, if blindsided. Always make eye contact with the person and say in a respectful voice:

"I need a moment to process what just happened."

"I hear that you feel I'm to blame. I'd like to take some time to regroup—and then discuss next steps later today."

"I'm completely taken aback by your reaction and need a moment to decide how I want to respond. Will you excuse me."

If something is said in the heat of the moment, it can't be taken back—
so remember, you're in control of your emotions and have the power to
choose how and when you respond.

COACHING CORNER

When were you blindsided, caught off guard, or blamed?

Given your understanding of responding versus reacting, how
could you have handled that situation differently?

Situation:

Original Response:

New Response:

Avoid Snap Reactions and Getting Angry

If you're someone who is prone to reacting out of emotion, here are some
strategies to practice on a regular basis:

- **Remind yourself of the age-old adage "Count to four before you roar!"**

- **Save emails to the "Draft" folder before sending them.**

- **Make a professional "PACT" with yourself.**

- **Do a self-inventory.** Be aware of *what* your hot buttons are, *who*
  gets under your skin, and *when* you're most annoyed (Is it when
  you're hungry? Or not prepared for a meeting?) Ask yourself,
  What's another interpretation of what just happened? Finding multiple meanings may be an alternative to taking it personally.

- **Express your hurt feelings in a diplomatic, tactful way.**

    "I'm concerned with what just happened."

    "I'm really upset by what you said."

    "This is unacceptable to me, and I'd like to circle back after I get more information."

- **Try the "perspective wall."** Think of the situation, or what the person said, and step back from it. Look at it from a distance, as if you were hearing about it from someone else. Does it change your perspective? Maybe it's not as bad as you initially thought when you were in the situation.

- **Divert your mind for a moment.** Think of your "happy place" or something that brings you a sense of calm. It's a temporary solution that over time may help you break the habit of reacting out of emotion.

- **Practice deep breathing.** Mentally focusing on your breath is a great way to distract the mind, relax the body, and buy your brain some time to think clearly. Research has shown that taking slow, deep breaths can calm you because the neurons in the brain tell the body it's time to relax.[4]

- **Pick your battles.** Some people and situations are drama—and not worth your energy or response. As the saying goes, "Breathe in, breathe out, move on."

Giving yourself time to process is not always easy—especially when leadership is involved. You owe it to yourself to take a moment—don't let someone else hold the pen to your story. You possess the power to make the choices that will progress your success.

The key is that the way you respond is a choice and not a reflex.

Another distinction to be aware of so that you can create an *accurate* impression of yourself is the difference between *commands* and *demands*.

3. *COMMANDS* VS. *DEMANDS*—
CONDESCENDING ATTITUDE

A participant in one of my recent workshops recounted a story of another class she had attended. The instructor tried to reconvene the class after a ten-minute breakout session by clapping her hands three or four times and firmly stating, "Everyone. Everyone." The participant shared that she felt immediately transported back to kindergarten—and that the instructor's actions and words were condescending.

Both demanding and commanding people *capture attention*; the difference is that one is perceived much more positively than the other. Whether through the voice or body, when someone demands your focus or action, it can be perceived as scolding, lecturing, or condescending. Conversely, some people naturally command attention because of how they appear and interact. They have the "it" factor—a high "likability quotient" to which people are naturally drawn. They're respectful and gracious—and because of this others *want* to look, listen, act, and answer.

COACHING CORNER

When you think of someone who naturally and immediately commands the attention of others, who comes to mind?

Do you command the attention of others?

What are some techniques that you have used, or seen others employ, to command the room?

Take a look at these top tips for how to more naturally command the attention and respect of others:

- Offer a sincere smile.

- Make meaningful eye contact.

- Have open and confident body language.

- Project your voice to be easily heard.

- Speak in a way that is substantive and impactful.

- Think about what you're projecting visually. Does your appearance substantiate your goal of commanding attention?

- Create value for listeners by speaking their "language."

- Consider how you can communicate your message so that it's of value to the other person. You'll immediately increase interest and engagement by using the WIIFT approach—"What's In It For Them."

- Be an effective listener by making others feel seen and heard—acknowledge their presence and actively listen to what they have to say.

As you continue on this professional development journey of creating an accurate impression, consider the subtle difference between being *assertive* and *aggressive*.

4. *ASSERTIVE* VS. *AGGRESSIVE*—ANGER

Have you ever been called aggressive, told you were abrupt or overly critical, or labeled as being too direct? Some aspect of your verbal or nonverbal communication may have seemed angry.

Both an assertive and an aggressive person may opt to take the lead, appear self-assured, and demonstrate initiative; the subtle difference is that aggressive people are also often perceived as being overly forceful, hostile, or creating conflict. The following questions will help you to understand why you may be perceived as aggressive rather than assertive.

- Do you have a *limited attention span* when others are talking—and lose focus quickly?

- Do you *talk fast*—and often without taking a breath?

- Are you *quick to take action*—or react out of emotion, rather than thoughtfully responding?

- Do you *interrupt* if you "get it"—not allowing the other person to finish the thought?

- Do you *lack empathy* because you're there to get ahead—not to "make friends?"

- Do you use "eraser words" such as *"But," "However," "That being said . . ."*—which could come across as discounting or dismissing what the other person said?

Over the years, I've had a number of clients ask for my help in appearing stronger, more confident—and "more aggressive." I've come to realize that many individuals associate showing initiative, and being a go-getter, with being aggressive—not realizing they're negatively labeling themselves—when there's a more positive option that reflects the same desired characteristics.

**The key is that other people's perceptions
of you are sometimes based on the qualities and
characteristics you claim to possess.**

There are a select number of industries, positions, and people that require, foster, and even reward an aggressive personality. If this applies to you, perhaps you've made a strategic decision to act or be perceived that way. If it's not an intentional choice, refrain from referring to yourself as aggressive.

You also want to be aware of being overly assertive. Being assertive is a "forward" communication style. It can be easily misperceived as overwhelming or overbearing to those who don't share this same self-assured, strong, and outgoing way of being. Using this tool too readily could inadvertently create the very perception that you were trying to avoid—being seen as aggressive.

When it comes to this particular pair of words, other concerns that surround them include:

> *"How do I soften my message so I am seen as assertive and not aggressive?"*

> *"If someone is constantly assertive, it can also be perceived as pushy."*

> *"How do you balance authority as a woman leader without sounding 'b*tchy'?"*

In an attempt to soften their messages so that they are not labeled as aggressive, many individuals undermine themselves. Some use "uptalk"—raising the pitch at the end of a sentence so that it sounds less declarative. This mitigates or softens the impact of a statement by making it sound more like a question. Many use "wimpy words" to hedge the directness of what they're saying, and still others make body language choices that give them a "smaller," less confident presence.

The key is not to sabotage yourself; it's about learning new techniques that can achieve the desired goal.

Here are key strategies for communicating assertively with diplomacy and tact:

- Smile.

- Speak concisely and in a charismatic way.

- Know your audience and use a similar style of delivery. Being mindful of pace, volume, and tone can prevent you from being seen as overwhelming or overly intense.

- Allow the assertiveness to come through your body instead of your voice—use the energy to exude open, approachable, confident body language.

- Invite others to share ideas, ask questions, and get involved in the conversation—this helps to establish that you're not lecturing or pushing your ideas on others.

- Refrain from always speaking first unless you're running the meeting—be conscious of varying when you give input. This will prevent others from assuming it's "all about you."

- Guide rather than "give"—help others to identify information or brainstorm a solution instead of giving the answer to them.

- Avoid repeating, overselling, or overexplaining your thought or position.

- Refrain from going into a meeting thinking you have to prove yourself.

- Challenge an idea—not the person.

- Avoid blaming.

- Eliminate "eraser words" such as *"On the other hand"* and *"Although."*

- Consider what you can do to help people feel that their needs matter to you—remember to focus on the value and "What's In It For Them" (WIIFT).

The key is to find the balance between knowing your audience and expressing yourself.

Having a voice, and being heard, is a very important topic for hundreds of people with whom I've interacted. It's a topic that many find difficult to address. One way to tackle this challenge is to highlight the difference between *interjecting* and *interrupting*.

5. *INTERJECTS* VS. *INTERRUPTS*— LACK OF ACKNOWLEDGMENT

"How do I get myself heard in a meeting?"

"People are constantly talking, then move on to another topic— I never get to say what I wanted."

"When someone is talking, I don't want to interrupt."

The acts of interjecting and interrupting are similar—both reflect someone inserting words into an existing conversation. While interjecting is perceived as a positive action, interrupting is often associated with a lack of self-awareness or self-restraint and seen as rude and disrespectful. The primary difference between the two actions is *acknowledgment*. When you acknowledge what people have said before inserting your own thoughts, they'll feel heard—and are more likely to appreciate your input. When people feel acknowledged, they also interpret actions and behaviors in a more positive way.

Next time you're at a meeting and want to participate in the conversation, consider the following strategies for interjecting:

- **Know when, and how, to speak up at meetings.**

  - Timing is important.

  - Look for, or create, a pause in the conversation—and then speak.

  - The impact of your message will be diminished if you speak over someone. Create the space to contribute.

- Avoid always being the first—or last—person to speak unless you're hosting the meeting; it can make what you say seem less impactful.

- Create opportunities to have a voice at the table. Ask to run the meeting or pose a question that others have to weigh in on—and then facilitate that discussion. Briefly summarize what someone else said—and then progress that thought by adding your opinion or contribution.

- **Avoid saying, "I'm sorry for interrupting."** Prefacing an interruption with an apology does not offset the act of interrupting. In most cases, the receiver is thinking, *If you're sorry, why are you doing it?* Plus, you've just negatively labeled yourself as an "interrupter." The simplest way to avoid both actions is to follow the "Interjecting Template" below.

The Interjecting Template will eliminate your impulse to apologize for having something to say. It will also create an environment to share your thoughts in a way that makes the other person feel acknowledged and respected. In addition, it's a diplomatic, tactful way to take the conversation back from a monopolizer. Practice the Interjecting Template when you want to skillfully break into the conversation.

The Interjecting Template

To use the Interjecting Template, follow these four steps:

- **Step #1: Say the speaker's name first.** Saying the speaker's name *first* creates a natural pause. When people hear their names, they often stop what they're doing and look, thereby creating a space for you to contribute to the conversation.

- **Step #2: Find a transition statement.** Look for an opportunity to build upon something the speaker has said that relates to what you want to say. People like to hear their ideas repeated—especially when it's associated with praise—because it gives them "verbal visibility": *"Ron, I'd also like to interject that in addition to the importance of an SOP manual for each department, another important factor is the timeliness of getting those manuals to the respective departments."*

- **Step #3: Share your thoughts in a clear and concise way.** *"I have a few ideas on how to streamline the process of getting SOP manuals to each department. My thought is we . . ."*

- **Step #4: End with appreciation.** Thank the speaker for letting you interject, both verbally and nonverbally (with an open hand— more on this in Chapter 3). Then turn the conversation back over to him or her. By combining the verbal with the nonverbal, you're sending a stronger message. *"Thanks, Ron (with an open hand gesturing toward Ron), for giving me the floor."*

The key to being seen as an interjector, versus an interrupter, is starting with acknowledgment and ending with appreciation.

The mere fact that you turned the conversation back over to the speaker will resonate many unspoken truths: that you are respectful, self-aware, gracious, and confident. There may be times when you do *not* want to give the conversation back to the speaker because he or she is monopolizing the conversation. If that's the case, take a look at the following strategies:

Taking Back the Conversation
from a Monopolizer

If the speaker is monopolizing the conversation, you may want to avoid turning the conversation back over to him or her after you've interjected. You have a brief opportunity to "save" the group. Turning the conversation over to a specific person in the room may end up throwing that person under the bus. This person may not be prepared to speak—or have anything to add.

The key is to turn the conversation back to the full group.

"Ron, you've brought-up a great topic. I'd like to open it up to the group (hands gesturing toward the group) *for thoughts on my idea—or for more ideas on how we can streamline the process of getting SOP manuals to each department."*

You have the power to progress your success and create the perception of yourself that you choose. Sometimes the perception that you choose for yourself, that you feel you've established, is not really the impression that others have formed. This is the case with our next pair of words—*passionate* and *emotional*.

To strongly believe in an idea, have a deep sense of conviction, or love what you do is an admirable level of commitment. How you communicate this level of commitment can be labeled as either passionate or emotional. Take a look at the distinction.

6. *PASSIONATE* VS. *EMOTIONAL*— UNFOCUSED ENERGY

Passion often has an innately positive connotation in the workplace, while being "emotional" generally carries a negative stigma—both reflect the *energy* carried within.

I'm fortunate to have a career that enables me to do what I love every day—helping others to communicate confidence, competence, and credibility in the professional arena—and in life. I've been told, "Wow, you're passionate." I internalize this statement to mean that people can see the energy and commitment that I consistently bring to what I do. There's also an underlying and more subtle interpretation—that for some, this energy may be overwhelming.

Throughout my interactions, I've learned that being passionate can be perceived differently depending on the audience as well as the way—and degree to which—I deliver that passion. If the receivers of your message don't share that same level of interest, commitment, urgency, belief, or enthusiasm, they may be turned off by your delivery and mislabel this positive display of energy as overly excited, reactive, or pushy. I looked for the differences in how passion was delivered—and noticed that when the energy behind the passion was focused and directed, it was perceived in a positive light. When the energy lacked focus, it was interpreted as emotional, which seemed to make the ideas being presented less impactful.

The key to reflecting focused energy is to include facts, make sure your delivery is substantive, and ensure your content is organized.

Harvard Business Review also captured research on passion from a gender perspective, with men responding that "unchecked emotion by women makes their ideas less convincing and compromised their credibility, because it focuses on style rather than content."[5] Finding the right balance between quality content and engaging delivery is important in being taken seriously and having the power to persuade others. It's important to stay authentic to your style while positioning what you say in a way that resonates with the audience.

To communicate passion rather than emotion, try the following techniques:

Do:

- Incorporate facts, numbers, or specific examples to support and progress your idea.

- Highlight the top three aspects of what you want to say instead of sharing a lot of examples.

- Use meaningful and deliberate hand gestures to further focus and support your verbal message.

- Pause periodically to reduce the perception of a lecture.

- Be intentional—have a focused plan for how you'll present your idea.

- Know your audience and What's In It For Them (WIIFT)—what resonates most and is of value to the listener?

- Align your goals with the team's, department's, or company's bigger vision.

- Rely less on your opinion and feelings and more on articulating key points to substantiate your message.

- Practice what you plan to say.

- Garner support for your idea *before* the meeting; this way you may not feel as if you have to prove your point—or yourself when it's your turn to speak.

- Check in with listeners and gauge the temperature of how they're receiving what you're saying by asking:

    "I'm interested to know your thoughts . . ."

    "How do you feel about what I've said?"

    "Is this a viable option the way you see it?"

- Add your idea to the agenda to underscore it visually.

- Present the content in a way that elicits questions, which allows you to indirectly emphasize key points and share information.

Don't:

- Rely solely on your commitment or enthusiasm to prove your point.

- Speak too loudly.

- Use large or constant hand gestures.

- Opt for body language that is too intense, such as standing when someone is sitting or leaning into an individual's personal space.

- Use emotional words.

- Take it personally when someone says, *"Relax"*—it's great feedback and insight that your delivery may need to be adjusted to the audience's style.

Once you share your thoughts, be prepared that you may receive a reaction other than the one you were expecting. Be mindful to remain composed and measured regardless of the response—passion can be misinterpreted in your delivery *and* response.

Another pair of words that warrants mentioning is *listens* and *hears*; they're used interchangeably and have distinctly different meanings.

7. *LISTENS* VS. *HEARS*—LESS PROCESSING

Individuals want to know that what's significant to them matters to you. On the surface, both listening and hearing reflect a similar action—the act of *receiving information*. The subtle difference between someone who's listening versus someone who's hearing is the *desire to process*. Great listeners have the sole goal of understanding *what* is being said, and they use multiple senses to do so. They realize there's time later to give advice, ask questions, and share thoughts. They're focused on truly being present and in the moment; they see their only action as processing the information being shared with them. Individuals who are merely hearing are using only their ears—they aren't actively engaged in internalizing what's being said.

> *Leaders who don't listen will eventually be surrounded*
> *by people who have nothing to say.*
> —ANDY STANLEY[6]
> Pastor and Founder North Point Ministries

COACHING CORNER

When did someone really listen to you?

Can you identify the subtle nuances of that interaction that resonated with you?

How would you rate yourself as a listener?

Fair	Good	Great	Skilled

**The key is to focus on what the speaker is saying,
the meaning behind his or her delivery, and the nonverbal
messages accompanying the speaker's words.**

Listening comes naturally to some. For most, it's a learned skill that takes practice. With all of the distractions that exist in this highly technical world, it's also a skill that takes commitment. While interacting with a variety of individuals, I've found listeners generally fall into four levels: passive, active, reflective, and empathic.

The Four Levels of Listening

Let's take a closer look into the four levels that define the art of listening.

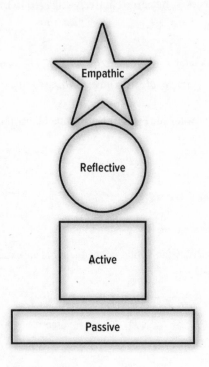

Passive Listening

Passive listening is what I consider to be "flat listening" or the lowest level of listening—with little to no energy being given to internalizing what someone is saying. You're there in body and not actively engaged in the process. Some consider it synonymous with hearing.

Active Listening

Active listening is a higher level of listening and can be characterized as showing engagement through both the voice and body. It also includes letting the speaker know you're in the moment.

Active listening actions may include:

- Listening for comprehension, *not* replying.

- Nodding occasionally to show understanding. Avoid constantly nodding, which can be distracting to the speaker, misperceived as being on autopilot, and seen as presumptive agreement if the speaker has not yet finished his or her thought.

- Sporadically interjecting statements of understanding.

- Asking clarifying questions and periodically summarizing or paraphrasing.

- Using nonverbal messaging to respond and show acknowledgment without interrupting the speaker.

- Ensuring your body language is receptive—facing the speaker fully, making eye contact, smiling when appropriate—and reflecting your undivided attention.

Research indicates that 90 percent of information transmitted to the brain is visual. The brain processes images 60,000 times faster than text. This is a critical detail as you consider the message that your body language is sending to the speaker.[7]

Nonverbal messaging is also a key aspect to the next level of listening—*reflective listening*.

Reflective Listening

Reflective listening builds on the actions of active listening and is demonstrated when the listener reflects back the essence of what's being said or expressed in voice, content, and body. Reflecting back someone's words or posture exactly, known as "mirroring," could be misinterpreted as mocking or be annoying to the speaker—especially if the speaker is upset or the situation is uncomfortable. Therefore, it's essential to make the distinction between mirroring and "paralleling"—which is to do something similar.

The key to paralleling is to reflect back something similar *in voice, content, and body.*

Let's take a more detailed look at the strategy of paralleling.

Paralleling

The purpose of paralleling is twofold. First, it conveys that on a deeper level you understand, and are in tune with, the *essence* of what the speaker is communicating—from the level of importance to the emotion around what's being said. Second, paralleling can help to create a comfortable environment for the speaker because you're making a concerted effort to speak this person's "language."

When you show that you understand what the speaker values (e.g., being able to vent without being given advice, respecting personal space) and that you understand this individual's communication style (e.g., using a quieter voice, sitting back in the chair versus leaning into the conversation), you are speaking this individual's "language" and he or she is more apt to be at ease around you and to feel heard and understood.

Examples of communicating a deeper understanding and speaking this person's "language" include:

- Reflecting the *essence* of the speaker's emotion, such as excitement or sadness, through facial expressions, tone of voice, and body language choices.

  - Avoid trying to match the speaker's emotion, which could escalate the situation and cause others to negatively label you.

  - Posture. If the speaker is sitting back, try to parallel this posture. If you were to lean forward into the speaker's personal space, it might be misperceived as too intense.

  - Facial expressions. If the speaker exhibits excitement, try to reflect the essence of that emotion. Neutral facial expressions, void of a smile or expressive eyes, could be misinterpreted as apathetic, uninterested, or judgmental.

- Using the *same key words* that the speaker expressed. You're strategically choosing to use the same key words as the speaker to reflect your understanding and to avoid being accused of putting words in the speaker's mouth. Capturing the speaker's feelings and emotion by using the same key words is vastly different from massively "mirroring" and copying everything the speaker says and does.

  Listener: *"I hear how <u>angry</u> you are."*

  If the speaker specifically said that he or she was "angry," then using that word would be the right choice. If the speaker said he or she was "upset" and you assumed that meant "angry," then your presumption could intensify the situation and antagonize the speaker.

- Avoid using the same key words the speaker expressed if they're inappropriate, derogatory, or bad-mouthing someone else.

- Avoid paralleling negative, extreme, or inappropriate behavior, such as using inappropriate language, showing anger, yelling, or exhibiting closed-off or hostile body language.

To parallel negative or inappropriate actions or expressions through emotion, voice, words, or body may create a misperception of you and could be misinterpreted by the speaker as negativity directed toward him or her.

COACHING CORNER

What is your level of commitment to being a more effective listener?

No time   Not my first priority   On my radar   Actively engaged

While training and traveling, I have found that many professionals consider the ability to exhibit empathy one of the distinguishing factors between a good communicator and a great communicator. It's also a key element in distinguishing an effective leader from a masterful one. This brings us to the highest level of listening—empathic listening.

Empathic Listening

In order to explore the *art* of empathic listening, it's essential that we highlight the core concept of empathy.

Empathy is the ability to understand someone's feelings on a deeper level and respond with compassion. This ability usually stems from having *experienced* the feelings or situation in one's own life. You can often reflect this deeper level of understanding by *naming* the specific emotion described, or feeling shown, by the speaker.

There's an important distinction to make, the difference between empathy and sympathy. Sympathy is feeling sorry for someone—which doesn't stem from a place of deep understanding or experience and may or may not lead to a show of compassion.

Marshall Rosenberg was a world-renowned psychologist whose life's work was focused on resolving conflict-ridden situations through the use of empathy. He believed that empathy had the power to diffuse conflict and also to increase understanding, patience, awareness, and peace. In his book *Nonviolent Communication: A Language of Life*, Rosenberg says that you "don't need to solve people's problems, you need to hear them"[8]— which brings us back to the topic of empathic listening.

Empathic listening is listening with a deeper level of understanding and show of compassion while incorporating all of the other listening levels.

Empathic listening actions include:

- Acknowledging, validating, or affirming what the speaker is saying. To do so, it's important to only say the word of *emotion* or *feeling* that was said or shown by the speaker, such as:

  "*I completely understand why you feel <u>frustrated</u>.*"

"I hear the _____ in your voice." (name the specific emotion)

"It sounds like what you would like is . . ."

"This must be incredibly difficult for you."

"I hear that what is most important to you is . . ."

"I'm here for you."

- Trying to broach, or encourage, conversation by using empathic starters, such as:

    "I hear the <u>sadness</u> in your voice. Would it help to brainstorm solutions?"

    "I'm sensing something is wrong. How can I help?"

    "I see your <u>frustration</u>—what can I do?"

    "I can see you're <u>aggravated</u>. Can you share with us some of the issues so we have a better idea of what exactly is bothering you?"

- Finding a way to stay actively engaged with the speaker—especially when the speaker is looking only to vent and not for a solution. Phrases include:

    "Tell me more."

    "What you're saying is very important."

    "What else can you share with me about . . . ?"

- Avoiding statements, such as:

    - *"It could always be worse."*

    - *"I know how you feel."*

    - *"You're overreacting."*

    - *"I told you."*

    - *"It's not that bad."*

- Avoiding putting words in the speaker's mouth by naming emotions they haven't said they feel.

- Avoiding indirectly bad-mouthing someone in your quest to show empathy and compassion:

  > Speaker: *"Bena is so aggressive. She can't have a rational conversation; she bullies others by yelling."*

  > Listener: (nodding) *"I hear you about Bena."*

Nodding is associated with agreement. In addition, those few words can quickly be misconstrued and taken out of context. As a result, the listener may appear to agree with the negative sentiment, which may not be the case. You can still be an empathic listener while staying true to your own feelings and opinions. Steer clear of head nodding and verbal affirmations when the speaker is referring to someone in a negative manner.

Showing empathy when someone *is* being negatively referred to requires increased awareness and a specific approach. Practice the following strategies so that you can refrain from engaging in negative conversations about others:

- Maintaining eye contact and keeping your head still.

- Staying silent. There will be other opportunities to share statements of affirmation and to show empathy. It doesn't need to be done in the moment that someone is being bad-mouthed.

- If the bad-mouthing persists and you're uncomfortable, try these phrases and then excuse yourself:

  > *"I can see you're <u>upset</u>. (Pause so the statement is heard as being sincere and not just a brush-off.) Let's catch up when things calm down for you."*

  > *"I can see you're <u>frustrated</u>. (Pause.) I hope things get better for you. I'll check in with you later."*

  > *"I can see you're <u>unhappy</u>. (Pause.) I hope your day improves."*

- Avoiding "eraser words" as they erase any positive or important sentiment that came before them. Some examples include:

    "I hear you, <u>but</u> . . ."

    "I understand how frustrated you are; <u>however</u> . . ."

    "It can't be easy. <u>That being said</u> . . ."

    By using eraser words, you remove or erase any reflection of empathy that came before. Avoiding the use of eraser words does not only pertain to showing empathy as a listener. The power of these words has a much longer reach into other areas, including during conversations, when giving feedback, in trying to persuade someone of an idea, and when complimenting others.

In your role as the listener, remember that the spotlight is *not* on you. It's very easy in your quest to reflect understanding and empathy to give examples and stories of when you experienced the same. Using "I" takes the attention off of the speaker. This can result in the speaker not feeling heard, getting frustrated, shutting down, or ceasing to confide in you altogether.

Increasing your awareness of the different levels of listening will help you to determine which level you want to engage—and with whom. You can't always reflect the highest level of listening, because not every situation or person requires or deserves that level of energy and commitment. In addition, even after practicing these strategies and making a concerted effort to be the most effective listener possible, you may still get distracted. Research reflects that there is a reason *why* we get distracted when listening.

Studies show that we listen at a rate of approximately 400 words per minute and speak at a rate of 125 to 250 words per minute.[9] If we listen at a faster rate than the speaker is talking, it makes perfect sense that we can become distracted. If the speaker has a tendency of speaking slower, or you process information at a faster rate than the average, that could create a "listening gap."

The Listening Gap

The listening gap is what I call that period of time during which the listener starts to zone out—the span between having heard and processed the information and the speaker still talking. It's during this time-frame that you want to proactively apply strategies to keep engaged and stay present with the speaker.

> ### COACHING CORNER
>
> What are your techniques for staying actively engaged as the listener even when you've already processed what the speaker is saying?

There are numerous reasons why listeners tune out, get distracted, grow frustrated, or lose interest. A major reason is that the speaker is long-winded—or conversely, too vague.

The key is to be a conscious and concise communicator.

As with every other pair of words, there is a subtle difference between being *concise* or *vague* that can make all the difference in how you're perceived.

8. *CONCISE* VS. *VAGUE*—NOT INFORMATIVE

If you can't explain it simply, you don't understand it well enough.
—ALBERT EINSTEIN
German-born physicist who developed
the theory of relativity

On the surface, both words represent an efficient way of communicating. The subtle line that differentiates someone who's vague from someone who's concise is the ability to be succinct while giving enough information that the listener feels *informed*. Getting quickly to what matters most to those listening will progress the perception that you're a concise, conscious, and credible communicator.

The key to communicating effectively up, down, and laterally—is to be informative and brief; it's to be concise.

Some strategies for being a concise communicator or helping someone else to be more informative and brief include:

- Applying the widely acclaimed acronym BLOT: Bottom Line On Top. Start with the "bottom line," or what's most important for the listener to know. Then continue with your explanation or communicating additional details

- Remembering a few of the trusted mantras that have spanned generations:

> *The most valuable of all talents is never using*
> *two words when one will do.*
> —THOMAS JEFFERSON
> Third president of the United States

> *Be Sincere; Be Brief; Be Seated.*
> —FRANKLIN DELANO ROOSEVELT
> 32nd president of the United States

> *Be Brief, Be Brilliant, and Be Gone!*
> —ORIGIN UNKNOWN

- Using the WIIFT strategy—What's In It For Them—determines what would be most valuable for the listener to hear. Then, BLOT it!

"What's In It For Them"

When you tailor your message to the priorities of the listener and position that information first, what you have to say instantly has more value. This strategy also reflects that you're a concise communicator because the listener is not waiting to hear the information he or she is interested in. To help organize your thoughts into WIIFT, consider three main drivers. These categories often become the lens through which others determine the value of what you're saying:

- **Results**—achieving outcomes and deadlines

- **Relationships**—focusing on people and building or sustaining rapport

- **Reputation**—considering how it makes the individual, team, leader, or organization look in the eyes of others

Being perceived as a concise communicator is reflected in your ability to succinctly share what's important to those listening. When in doubt about the essence of their interest, try:

- **Asking:**

  - *"When it comes to _____, what specifically can I share with you?"*

  - *"There are three key areas that may be of interest to you when it comes to _____. Where would you like me to start?"*

  - *"To make the most of our time, what is the most important aspect for you that I can address?"*

- **Considering:**

  - Why the content is important to them

- What their level of knowledge is around the subject

- Which aspect of what you're saying will resonate most with them

- **Listening:**

  - For specific questions or comments that will give you insight into areas of interest or priorities

  - To interjections that may help you to redefine your core talking points

The key is that the listener is given enough information to ask questions or delve deeper into the conversation—and that the information presented is succinct and informative.

When communicating, another way to reflect this competence and credibility is through your ability to *refer* to information—and not *read* it word-for-word.

9. *REFERS* VS. *READS*—LACK OF CONFIDENCE

Unless you're reading an exact quote, text, or statistic, avoid reading your material to the listener. It severely undermines your credibility because you're communicating a sense of nervousness, uncertainty, discomfort, and lack of competence. It seems as if you don't know the information well enough to speak about it. Reading from a paper or screen can also prevent you from making meaningful eye contact with the audience or your conversation partner. The audience will forgive you for many things—they'll be hard-pressed to form a positive impression of you, as the speaker, if you're not looking at them.

When you're prepared and have organized what you want to say, you can feel confident—there's a structure to your content. This structure allows you to speak in an organized fashion while having some freedom for how you get to the different points. The outcome—you can refer to your notes with no need to rely on them. Having a structure is different from being scripted, which could come across as insincere, robotic, or reflecting nervousness.

To master the art of *referring* to your notes, practice these techniques:

- Convert your message into a few key bullet points.

- Place key pictures or words throughout your slide deck to trigger your thoughts.

- Write reminder notes in the margin.

- Circle, underline, bold, or highlight key words.

- Videotape yourself so that you can see what you're verbally and visually communicating to others.

- Practice without your notes so that your voice sounds engaging and not monotone.

- Avoid memorizing the bulk of your information so that you're not afraid of deviating from the "script."

- Avoid reading your opening and closing remarks—which are two great opportunities to connect with your audience.

Sometimes you don't have the luxury of time, or advance notice, to prepare or tailor your ideas. This requires that you organize your thoughts and find your words instantaneously. For many, this is nerve-racking and creates a challenge in discerning what should be said and delivering that information in a succinct manner.

Speaking extemporaneously is the ability to speak off the cuff, unplanned, and spontaneously. Practice using the Extemporaneous Structure model when you're put on the spot and want to communicate concisely.

Extemporaneous Structure

- **Step #1: Offer both nonverbal and verbal acceptance.** Respond with confident eye contact, smile—if appropriate, use his or her name, and offer verbal acceptance.

    "Sure, Joan, happy to share where we are on the client proposal."

- **Step #2: Share three to five key points.** Provide three to five points to support your answer and determine them by asking yourself, *What's most important for this person to hear that would reflect my grasp of the subject, fulfill his or her need for information, or communicate that I have the issue under control?*

    "There are three key points to highlight. We met the January first deadline to get the proposal to the client; they seemed very happy and will revert back in two weeks. The team is already preparing for the two options we anticipate the client will choose. This way, we can stay two steps ahead and quickly turn around any requests from the client."

- **Step #3: Give a closing or actionable statement.** Conclude on a positive note. You can briefly tie everything back to the original question and/or ask if there's any further information you can share.

    Closing statement: *"So that's the latest update, Joan, on the client proposal."*

    Actionable statement: *"That is a brief glimpse, Joan, into where we are with the client. Would you like me to put something more specific together for you and email it later today?"*

The key is to remain calm, positive, and speak in a measured, concise way so that you reflect confidence and credibility.

It's important to put your energy toward the audience, your delivery, and the quality of your content—and not to be remembered for reading. You are only as interesting as you are interested. Focus your energy outward instead of inward or downward. This will allow you to be perceived as persuasive and engaging.

As you increase your awareness of the subtle differences between similar words and the potential impact those nuances have on how you're perceived, a pair of words for which the line is easily blurred is being *friendly* and being *friends*.

10. *FRIENDLY* VS. *FRIENDS*— BLURRING BOUNDARIES

In the professional arena, there are delicate balances that need to be maintained—to be people-focused while being task-oriented, to achieve results without stepping on toes, to bring technical savvy to a situation without overcomplicating the explanation, and, for many, to be friendly without being friends.

If you're in a leadership position or maintain a critical role where neutrality is key, being mindful of treating everyone professionally and similarly, to the extent possible, is essential. Work relationships matter—and are a large part of enjoying your work environment. Just as getting goals accomplished, solving problems, and diffusing tension are essential elements to success, so is building rapport with the individuals with whom you work. The danger in building rapport is the minute you treat one person in a friendlier way or more favorably than another, resentment may form as some people start to wonder why they're not receiving the same treatment or benefits as others. If you take one of your direct reports to lunch or go regularly for drinks with a few, excluding others, you may be labeled as someone who plays favorites. Your actions and decisions as a leader may start to be questioned, scrutinized, or implemented begrudgingly.

The key when it comes to quality interactions with your direct reports is to try to make everyone around you feel equal.

It's also important to be friendly with your own managers. Again, the minute you blur this boundary and shift into the "friends" zone, your intentions might be questioned. Some may start to wonder, *are you trying to get into their good graces for the sole purpose of advancement?* This behavior could also create jealousy or dissension among the team and create an unpleasant, uncomfortable work environment.

The key when it comes to quality interactions with your leadership is to build rapport while maintaining professionalism.

In this highly connected, technology-driven world, social media—specifically Facebook and Instagram—have complicated matters by creating platforms that often assist in blurring these boundaries.

COACHING CORNER

Have you been on a team where one of your team members was friends with the boss? If so, how did it make you feel?

As a leader, have you ever blended the boundaries and formed a friendship with one of your direct reports?

Yes   No

If so, as you look closer at the situation, were there any negative responses or repercussions stemming from that choice?

What are your thoughts on this topic?

Social Media and Boundaries

With instant invites and easy access to each other's personal lives, many employees and leaders find themselves in a complicated and awkward situation when sent an invite—to connect or not to connect. If you work in a social media–driven industry, for a tech company, or within a department that utilizes internal pages and accounts, it may be common company practice, and even encouraged, that you accept. In general, it's best to keep your personal life separate from your professional world.

- If you don't want to connect on social media, you could *say* the following when someone sends a request:

  "My New Year's resolution is to focus on my work/life balance. So I'm keeping Facebook for personal and LinkedIn for work. Are we connected on LinkedIn?"

Or instead of accepting a Facebook invite, you can simply reply:

  "Are we connected on LinkedIn?"

This professionally driven approach lets you avoid having to decline the invitation while quickly turning the focus of the conversation to a positive option by suggesting another way to achieve the goal of connecting.

- If invited, you could *create* an option: If you want to keep your personal life separate from your professional world without the fear of offending your boss, colleagues, or direct reports, an option is to create a new social media profile. This profile would exist for the sole purpose of connecting you to colleagues.

One important way to build rapport—especially with your leadership, is to add value. It's essential that you know your value and are able to articulate how that value benefits them. This is the distinction between our next pair of words—*self-promotes* and *brags*.

11. *SELF-PROMOTES* VS. *BRAGS*— NO CONNECTION TO WIIFT

Professional boxer, activist, and philanthropist Muhammad Ali once said, *"If you can back it up, it's not bragging."* And, while true, not everyone is comfortable talking about themselves—much less promoting themselves. Through my years of coaching, I've learned that one of the biggest reasons people don't speak about themselves is that they're afraid *"It will sound like I'm bragging."* It won't sound that way if you put as much importance on *how* you structure the information as you do on *what* you share.

COACHING CORNER

Are you comfortable speaking about yourself and your accomplishments?

Yes   No

Self-promotion is the ability to articulate your value and how that value benefits others. It's *other-focused*. Bragging is to boast about your achievements or inflate yourself to others, sometimes without validity; often with bragging, there is no consideration for "What's In It For Them." It's *self-focused*.

This topic also raises the question, if you never, or rarely, speak about yourself, how does someone know the value that you bring? Why would your senior leadership know who you are? What would be the reason to approve a raise, assign you to an important project, or view you as a resource in a certain skill area? One way to give yourself "verbal visibility" and share your capabilities with others is through a Credibility Statement.

Credibility Statement

When introducing yourself, there are two key aspects that you want to include—statements that quickly reflect the value that you bring, along with information that helps listeners to ask questions or continue the conversation. You want to reflect competence, establish yourself as a valuable part of the team, and be remembered for being other-focused. An introduction that achieves these outcomes is referred to as a Credibility Statement.

Preparing your Credibility Statement is an important part of self-promotion and creating verbal visibility. It will empower you to speak up in a professional and value-added way—all without feeling as if you're bragging or need to "pass" because you don't know what to say. Some of the details you want to consider when creating a Credibility Statement include:

- **Keep it concise.** Aim to speak for 30 to 60 seconds, or four or five sentences. Knowing you'll be speaking only for mere seconds may help to take the edge off about speaking publicly about yourself—or wondering how long it should last.

- **Keep it simple.** Clearly articulate what you do—especially if you work in an industry, such as IT, digital media, engineering, finance, science, or law. In highly technical fields, preconceived notions exist that many professionals have a difficult time explaining what they do without getting into complex concepts or using confusing jargon.

- **Watch word choice.** Choose substantive, impactful words over weaker words, such as: "I lead," "I direct," "I spearhead," and "I'm in charge of" rather than "I oversee" or "I manage."

- **Think about the WIIFT.** Similar to a cover letter, which needs to be tailored to the recipient and highlight the most pertinent key points, you want your Credibility Statement to reflect the value that you bring to the listener—thereby encouraging him or her to want to know more and remember you.

It's also important to highlight the difference between a Credibility Statement and an "elevator pitch." An elevator pitch generally markets the value of a product, idea, or service. A Credibility Statement markets *you*—and the value that you bring to the position or project. If you don't have one, it's time to create it.

Example Credibility Statement

"Good morning. My name is Laura Joan Katen. As a communications speaker, I travel over 100 days a year helping individuals to communicate confidence, competence, and credibility in 4 core areas. As the founding partner of KATEN CONSULTING, my core focus is sharing strategies for projecting a powerful presence through voice and body. I look forward to being a resource for you and to our working together."

When it comes to creating your Credibility Statement, there are six key steps to keep in mind.

- **Step #1: Give a greeting.** Including a greeting at the start of your Credibility Statement acknowledges others, reflects that you're at ease, and helps to create a conversational tone. In certain environments, *"Hi"* and *"Hello"* may be seen as too casual. It's personal preference as to the tone you want to set.

- **Step #2: State your full name.** If there's even one person in the group whom you don't know, introduce yourself with both your first and last name. Placement of your name is best said up front.

  While giving a keynote talk recently at a client's annual conference, I gained additional insight into the value of using full rather than only first names when meeting someone. When being introduced to the chief information officer, I had introduced myself using my full name. Later, when he and I were speaking, it appeared he was at a loss for my name. After a brief pause, he said, "Katen." In that moment, I realized that people's brains weigh, value, and remember information differently. Had I only shared my first name, he may never have recalled it, and the conversation that was connecting us may have been cut short. For some reason the name *Katen* stood out to him—and was the vehicle that allowed us to keep building rapport.

Using your full name will also help to set a professional tone, distinguish you from someone else with the same first name, and make it easier to associate who you are with what you do for the company.

- **Step #3: Mention your title, current role, and company name.**

  - *Title.* Include it after your name, especially if it's unique, distinguishes you, or is prestigious. If it's less substantive than other information you're including or doesn't reflect the job that you do, my suggestion is either to not include it or add it to the end of your statement.

  - *Current core responsibility.* Place it at the beginning, since this information immediately reflects your value. Listeners' attention spans are limited, so avoid wasting those initial moments when the audience is most engaged.

  - *Company name.* While optional, finding a way to refer to your company name could make your statement seem less generic.

- **Step #4: Front-load engaging information.** Place engaging, valuable information in the beginning of your statement. In addition, focus on including important numbers, which for many listeners make what you do more memorable than a statement consisting solely of words. Engaging information includes:

  - Large territory or region (e.g., in charge of North America and Canada)

  - Prestigious client or important project (e.g., working on Disney+)

  - Unique responsibility or role (e.g., archives coordinator or scientist working on a cure for a specific disease)

- Impressive fact such as:

  > Money (e.g., *". . . thereby helping the company to earn 12 million dollars in revenue from the Asian Equities Conference our department hosted."*)

  > Numbers (e.g., in charge of 200 employees or part of an 8-person team)

  > Years at company, experience, or time in the industry or position (If you've only been in the position for a year or less, make sure to also include more substantive information that reflects your overall experience and expertise—such as your years in the industry.)

  > Education and degrees (You may want to include your qualifications if they showcase your value or you have a job where credentials make a difference.)

  > Company or department goal (If you're helping to achieve a specific companywide or interdepartmental goal, sharing your role in that initiative will help to reflect that you're currently progressing the business forward and are in tune with the priorities of the company.)

- **Step #5: WIIFT statement.** This is the key detail that will help differentiate you from being seen as someone who's bragging—how your value *benefits others*. Therefore, the content will likely change as the audience changes—and the information you choose to include will evolve and shift with your professional growth and goals. Make the connection with how your role and responsibilities matter to the organization. One way to achieve this is to offer to be a resource or lend your expertise to a particular challenge or task.

- **Step #6: Closing statement.** You opened your Credibility Statement with a greeting, and now you want to end it with a closing. Try:

"I look forward to working with you."

"Good to meet everyone."

"Thank you for having me."

"It's a pleasure to be here."

"I look forward to contributing to the success of the project and our organization."

Your Credibility Statement is business-formal. It's geared toward those you interact with *internally* at the company, because it may be highly technical, jargon-based, or business-focused, and it's tailored to the specific work audience, situation, or environment. You can also tweak it so that it's appropriate for your social interactions and events, such as a networking event or dinner party.

The key is not to sound scripted—especially in social situations. Focus on communicating what you do in a more conversational, relatable manner.

COACHING CORNER

After learning about the importance of communicating your value to others and the difference between self-promotion and bragging, use the space below and the strategies shared to write your Credibility Statement.

Greeting:

Full Name:

Title, Current Role, and Company Name:

Key Statements: *(Remember to front-load what's most important / impressive to the listener.)*

WIIFT Statement:

Closing Statement:

Once you've created your Credibility Statement, time yourself. Your goal is to be able to share what you do, in a way that reflects your value and engages the listener, in ideally 45 seconds while speaking at a measure pace. Ready?

The goal of this book is to offer another perspective for approaching your communications that will progress your success. Knowing the distinct differences between very similar words can help you to distinguish yourself, reflect confidence, clarity, and credibility, and create an *accurate* impression of you.

YOUR QUESTIONS ANSWERED

1. *"How do you find the balance between sharing too little and too much information?"*

   - Tailor your content to the listener—WIIFT.

   - Add a visual. Research has shown that we remember approximately four times greater what we see than what we hear. Visuals can be used to engage, clarify, and make information meaningful.

- Think of a breaking news report—too little information and you give viewers vague information so that they can't speak about the story. Too much information and the story may become boring to viewers.

2. *"Do you always have to give a full Credibility Statement? Sometimes I'm in a meeting and people are only giving their names and titles."*

Personal preference, situational awareness, and context always come into play. You have to gauge what's appropriate for the situation. There are times you'll want to give a full Credibility Statement—especially if some key players with whom you get limited visibility are there. Other times, you may opt for an abridged version of your statement because it's more in line with the tone or pace of the meeting.

3. *"I often deflect praise because it makes me uncomfortable, but after taking your session I now know that's undermining. How can I handle this more effectively going forward?"*

It's not always easy to accept a compliment. This discomfort could come from reasons in your "Invisible Backpack" (more on that in Chapter 5) or because you're not sure what to respond.

To respond graciously and professionally, try the following techniques:

- Say, *"Thank you."* or *"Thank you for noticing."*

- Avoid minimizing or countering the compliment:

  Compliment: *"You did a really good job on that client proposal."*

  Minimizing response: *"Oh, that was nothing."*

  If you downplay your accomplishments or refute praise too many times, it may stop coming altogether. Others may start to wonder if you really do deserve the credit or question your abilities and self-confidence.

- Grab a glass of wine or cup of coffee and take a moment to list your strengths and the things you do very well. This internal acknowledgment will better prepare you for graciously accepting others' recognitions and external praise.

- Step up, step out, or step over—your choice. There are professionals who will always step up. They are persistent, they will rise to the challenge, or they will accept an outcome with gravitas. Part of rising to the occasion is stepping outside of your comfort zone—which can include graciously accepting praise. This is much more favorable than those who step out; they choose not to engage, don't want to be involved, or feel they are not capable. Finally, there are individuals who step over. They will bully, steal credit, or do whatever it takes regardless of the impact it has on others. Add your name to the list of people who step up.

- Ask for feedback periodically. Praise is feedback. Even though it's positive, it could still be uncomfortable if you're not used to regularly receiving feedback. Request it from someone who you trust, respect, and has the perspective to give accurate feedback. Position your request as wanting balanced feedback—both strengths and opportunities for improvement, so that you gain a well-rounded view.

4. *"If I am the speaker, what can I do to better hold someone's attention?"*

In this chapter, the role of the listener was highlighted. Let's turn the tables—to the speaker.

- Prepare visuals to support what you're saying, such as handouts, a Prezi or PowerPoint presentation, props, 3-D models, or videos.

- Be interactive by utilizing flip charts or a game based learning platform such as Kahoot!

- Focus on body language, vocal delivery, and word choices that engage the listener.

- Turn the page—and you'll find the next two chapters are dedicated to addressing your question.

The core concept behind making an accurate impression is to know how you want to be perceived and to be aware of what you may be doing to support or undermine that perception. Your body language plays a significant role in the perception that others form of you and is the main element that we'll explore in the next chapter.

CHAPTER THREE

PROJECTING CONFIDENCE
AND PRESENCE

Fake it until you become it.
—AMY CUDDY
American social psychologist

Your body language can instantly help or quietly hinder the impression you want to make. In addition, the core of being seen as an effective communicator is the perception that *other people* have of you. Therefore, this chapter will increase your awareness of important nonverbal messaging so that you can quickly and consciously project confidence and executive presence through your body.

Do you communicate confidence?

COACHING CORNER

Circle the answers that best describe you.

1. Do you move at a measured pace?

   Never   Occasionally   Always

2. Do you make meaningful eye contact?

   Never   Occasionally   Always

3. Do you make yourself "smaller" in presence through body language choices?

Never   Occasionally   Always

4. Does your attire reflect careful consideration and attention to detail?

Never   Occasionally   Always

5. Do you keep your hands in the Conversation Zone—the space ideal for gesturing? (More on that later.)

Never   Occasionally   Always

6. Do you smile regularly?

Never   Occasionally   Always

7. When you sit, do you take up space and have a visual presence?

Never   Occasionally   Always

What is the perception that others have of you at work?

COACHING CORNER

Circle any phrases that others may use to describe you.

Appears confident

Looks angry or annoyed

Arm crosser or hand clasper

Thoughts show on face

Looks unapproachable

Not a good listener

Fidgets when uncomfortable

Positive demeanor and attitude

As you review both assessments, take note of your strengths as well as areas that may be undermining you—or impacting your message.

There are three main ways we communicate when face-to-face. We'll delve deeply into two of them (vocal delivery and words) in the next chapter. For now, let's take a closer look at nonverbal communication and what you are silently saying through your "physical language."

The primary nonverbal components include:

- Facial expressions

- Hand gestures

- Posture

- Movement

These elements can instantly impact the message you send about yourself and communicate to others. Therefore, it's important to highlight how each can reflect or undermine confidence, approachability, and trustworthiness.

FACIAL EXPRESSIONS

Facial expressions are a key factor in nonverbal communication. Two important expressions at the top of the list are eye contact and smiling.

Eye Contact

When you're in a culture, business environment, or among individuals who expect and respect eye contact, it's essential to make *meaningful* eye contact. This important nuance helps you to establish a connection with someone, build rapport, communicate trustworthiness, and reflect confidence. It's important to get comfortable making eye contact so that your eyes don't reveal your uneasiness while presenting or during conversations.

Tips and techniques to make more meaningful eye contact include the following:

- Keep your head still, which is often perceived as calm, focused, and thoughtful eye contact.

- Maintain eye contact for three or four seconds, or a few sentences, before looking away—the timing needs to feel natural.

- Hold eye contact a bit longer if you or the other person wears glasses; glare on glasses can make it harder to tell if eye contact is being made.

- If speaking to a group or to keep nerves to a minimum, start by looking at a friendly face. Then periodically reconnect with that "safe face" throughout your speech or presentation.

- When giving a presentation to a larger crowd, view the audience as the letter W. The goal is to look at someone sitting in the left back of the audience, front, back center, front, and right back. This will help to ensure that you're not focusing on only one person.

Another important facial expression and one that can quickly show approachability is a smile.

Smiling

Has anyone ever called you aggressive, intimidating, or too direct? A *sincere* smile can do wonders in balancing that perception. A sincere smile reflects warmth and confidence and helps others to feel comfortable around you—which is a key element to your success.[1] It's also important to be authentic so the smile doesn't come across as forced, sarcastic, or snide.

HAND GESTURES

We also send significant messages through our hand gestures, which is one way individuals express energy, focus their thoughts, and gain insights into others. There are some people who refer to themselves as "hand-talkers" because they constantly gesticulate. There's also a cultural aspect to consider, as hand gestures are an integral part of verbal communication for many nationalities. Others manifest their inner nervousness through unconscious hand habits. Still there's a fourth group of individuals who do nothing with their hands, which makes them appear too stiff.

In general, poses where hands touch can create a visual barrier between the speaker and the audience, and make an individual look "smaller" in presence.

It's very unlikely that you would hear someone say any of the following:

- *"When my boss crosses her arms, I feel she is much more connected to the team."*

- *"When my colleague stands with her right hand grabbing on to her left wrist, she looks completely confident."*

- *"When my direct report is giving a presentation and keeps passionately pointing at people, he reflects approachability."*

These poses reflect the polar opposite of connectivity, confidence, or approachability. A few subtle shifts can make all the difference in exhibiting body language that is open and self-assured.

Subtle Shift #1: Hands Don't Touch

It's important to clarify that *hands don't touch* means they can touch momentarily—not stay connected. Poses where hands stay connected, such as clasped in front of or behind the body, crossed over the chest, or hidden in pockets, can make the body look closed off and signify vulnerability, aggression, or discomfort.

The key is to concentrate on maintaining open body language—unless it's a deliberate choice.

One way to maintain open body language is to keep your hands in the "Conversation Zone."

The Conversation Zone

Imagine an invisible box in the center of the body that goes from chest to belly button, ribs to ribs. It's called the "Conversation Zone" or "Conversation Box." When gesturing, focus on keeping your hands around the space of the invisible box. If you use very large gestures, it could be overwhelming and intimidating. For onlookers, not privy to the conversation, it could appear that you're being aggressive or yelling. If you use tiny gestures positioned below or inside this invisible box, the audience may not be able to see them and you could appear uncomfortable, and unconsciously make yourself look "smaller" in presence.

In addition to the Conversation Zone, there are two techniques that I recommend using to keep your hands from undermining you:

Technique #1: Use Deliberate Gestures

Use deliberate, specific hand gestures that support your verbal message. Some ways to achieve this include:

- Making comparisons:

    Left hand palm up = *"Let's talk about the revenue in Q1 . . ."*

    Right hand palm up = *". . . versus the revenue in Q2."*

- Showing height, width, or length

- Enumerating an agenda list in the air

- Using your fingers to emphasize key points or numbers

- Demonstrating the start and end points by moving both hands simultaneously in a palms-up horizontal motion

- Outlining an image in the air

By choosing intentional and meaningful hand gestures, you create a visual picture for the listener that supports what you're saying. This strategy can help to increase interest, the rate of comprehension, and engagement. It's also an excellent way to avoid letting your nervous energy manifest into fidgeting or other undermining mannerisms, such as playing with your wedding band, that may distract your listener or detract from your message.

Technique #2: Keep a Professional Anchor in Your Hand

A professional "anchor" is something that has a hard, firm structure, such as a clipboard, hard cover spiral notebook, binder, legal pad, or padfolio. Similar to a ship's anchor, this professional anchor weighs down and stills one side of your body. The purpose is to help you maintain open body language, channel excess nervous energy, and have a professional way to refer to your notes. Anchors can help you to appear more confident when giving a presentation in front of a group and avoid low power postures while seated.

When standing, the anchor can rest inside the crook of your elbow, held by that hand—upright and comfortably near the body. Alternatively, you can place the anchor in the web of your hand and let it hang down along the body. Be conscious not to place the anchor in front of your body or "hug" it by bringing both arms around it. This could result in an undermining posture—it may appear that you're uncomfortable and hiding behind a visual barrier.

Depending on the formality of your meeting and the context that requires you to use an anchor, holding a cup of coffee or bottle of water may be appropriate and do the trick of keeping your body open and lessening your nervousness. In addition, if you're giving a presentation, a great option for an anchor is the presentation clicker.

There are a few items to *avoid* when selecting an anchor:

- **Insignificant items.** Index cards, individual pieces of paper, or a small notebook are not going to look as substantive or have the same effect in keeping your body language open and "weighing down" or stilling your body.

- **Technology.** In this technology-driven world, it's very common to have a cell phone in hand and a laptop or iPad with us throughout the day. Technology has also become synonymous with being distracted. Even when using your laptop to take notes while in a meeting, those around you may still wonder in the back of their minds, *"Is he really taking notes or just checking and responding to emails during our meeting?"* Add to the equation that all anyone wants from you is to be seen and heard, and suddenly there are misperceptions and hurt feelings.

Refrain from using technology as an anchor; it can make others feel that they're competing for your attention. When someone feels unimportant or less than, it can be strong enough to change the way they perceive and interact with you.

- **Pen.** If you're uncomfortable while speaking or presenting, it's best not to hold a pen as your anchor. Any nervous energy may result in unconscious clicking. This is usually very annoying to others, and it distracts your audience from focusing on what you're saying. In addition, you may also end up unconsciously pointing it at someone, which can be very off-putting.

This brings us to our next subtle shift that can help you to reflect confidence through your body and, at the same time, build rapport with others.

Subtle Shift #2: Using an Open Hand

If you want to be seen as more diplomatic and tactful, use an open hand instead of a pointed finger when gesturing to someone—or something. The subtle messaging of an open hand is inclusivity and careful consideration not to offend.

I've noticed that when gesturing to others, the majority of people point. Throughout my talks, when someone broaches the topic of body language and gestures, I ask the audience how being pointed at makes them feel. The response is always similar: they comment about their "personal space," that they want to "withdraw," or that they feel "alienated," "annoyed," or "singled out."

In most cases, pointing is an innocent gesture. It's also where one person's intention can be another's misperception, since for many it's considered an aggressive mannerism that can contradict a positive or well-intentioned phrase or question. Contradicting messages can really diminish your impact—and can quickly create miscommunications and barriers to building rapport. It's essential that your nonverbal "language," what you say, and how you sound are all consistent in order to deliver the most accurate, effective message—and so that others feel comfortable interacting with you.

COACHING CORNER

In thinking about the nonverbal "language" that you speak, are there any subtle shifts to your facial expressions or hand gestures that could help make someone feel more comfortable around you?

POSTURE

The third critical element of body language is your posture—and how you carry your body.

When Superman comes out of the phone booth to save the world, he doesn't scrunch his body inward. Imagine if he declared, *"I'm going to save the world!"* with shoulders hunched, head lowered, hands together, and feet crossed. He opens himself up to appear bigger and more "powerful" by taking up space, standing tall with shoulders back, placing fists on hips, positioning legs strong and firm, and holding his head high. Your posture and physical presence is a key element of the impression you project and is incredibly important to the perception that others form of you.

Everyone has internal energy. If allowed to run rampant, without a clear and specific plan for use, this energy may manifest in unintentional outward displays of nervousness or discomfort. Left unaddressed, these unconscious tendencies may become negative mannerisms or habits that undermine you. Let's look at some different ways you can shift your posture so that you appear more confident, in control, and engaged.

Standing

Standing tall, with shoulders back, feet firmly planted, and weight evenly distributed reflects confidence. People looking at you have no idea that you may be uncomfortable or nervous unless you "tell" them through your body.

When standing, the same concept regarding "hands don't touch" can be applied to the legs. I refer to the posture of standing with one leg crossed over the other as "pretzel legs." Unless posing for pictures, consistently defaulting to this posture can make you look "smaller" in presence and undermine your impact. Other stances to avoid, which often stem from unconscious discomfort or nervous energy, include:

- Leaning on one hip
- Ankles touching, creating a much narrower stance or base
- Shifting the body constantly or swaying
- Fidgeting feet
- Standing stiff

Standing Still vs. Standing Stiff

Standing still exudes an innate comfort and ease, reflects focused energy, and shows command over the body until you have reason to move. This helps the body to stand tall, keeps it actively engaged, and allows the listener to focus on the content of what you're saying. There are no visual distractions. Standing stiff reflects discomfort, nervousness, and awkwardness of the body—and is often revealed through stilted movement, tension in the body, and a look of formality.

To reflect open and confident posture and avoid undermining your presence, one technique is to practice the concept of "Power Posing."

Power Posing

According to social psychologist Amy Cuddy, holding a position of power for around two minutes can create the impression that you appear more confident.[2]

Having practiced this art of Power Posing myself, I agree with the fundamentals of the technique. It calms my mind and body, centers my internal energy, and helps me to exude a composed, focused demeanor that reflects competence, confidence, and credibility. Start with a stance slightly less than shoulder-width apart, weight evenly distributed on both legs, make two fists and place them on your hips—which creates the "wing" arm formation (you want your "wings" to be firmly pointed straight out on the sides of your body), and stand tall with head high.

Since Cuddy presented her conclusions on Power Posing, there's now some debate around the validity of the research. Whether you agree or disagree with the merits of her research, try Power Posing before an important meeting, speaking engagement, or nerve-racking negotiation. See if it changes your mindset and your body and makes a difference for you.

COACHING CORNER

Which situations make you feel nervous?

With whom do you need to feel most confident?

What is your go-to strategy for getting into a positive mindset and exuding confidence?

Saying a mantra is also part of what helps to prepare my mind and body when I am Power Posing. The goal of your statement, of these powerful words—this self–pep talk of sorts, is to inspire you to be your best, most confident self. When creating your mantra, put it into a positive context, such as:

"I got this."

"I can do this because I've done it before and it went great."

"Get in the game. Come on, you own this. This is yours."

Avoid including negative words, or what you are *not* going to do:

"This is no problem."

"I'm not gonna worry."

"I can't focus on anything bad right now."

You want your mind and body surrounded by positive self-talk and statements of affirmation and validation. Hold your pose for the length of time you need to feel a surge of control, calm, and confidence, while you think of or say your mantra.

**The key is to remember that the body responds
to what the mind thinks.**

COACHING CORNER

What is your mantra?

What could you say to get your body and mind into a confident place?

Does Power Posing work for you?

Sitting

Similar to standing, your posture while seated can communicate a great deal—as can *where* you sit.

Body Positioning

- Avoid slouching or appearing too casual—you can shift slightly forward so you're not resting against the back of the chair.

- It's optimal to sit about a foot back from the edge of the table—that's approximately the distance between your wrist and elbow. This space prevents you from being stuck behind a visual barrier and gives you more of a presence because more of you can be seen.

- Depending on what's most comfortable for you, plant your feet firmly on the ground or cross your legs. Crossing your legs upright can often force you to sit upright, which may be perceived as very formal. Try crossing your legs and then slanting them in one direction for a more relaxed posture that still allows you to look engaged.

- Maintain "hands don't touch" by either using the armrests or placing an anchor, such as a notebook or coffee cup, on the table in front of you. By placing an anchor within arm's reach, you are intentionally and intermittently providing another point of focus for your hands besides your lap. This can help you to remain open, still, and engaged and keep clasped hands out of your lap.

Seat Choice and Placement

- Arrive early to a meeting so you can select the seat you want, build rapport by chatting with a few people as they enter, or exchange a quick update before the meeting begins.

- Avoid corner or wall seats as they are poor for visibility and can exclude you from the flow of conversation.

Presence by Proximity

- Find opportunities to sit next to a leader, superstar performer, or key player as this can project prestige simply from your proximity.

Seat Quality and Height

- If your chair is adjustable, raise the seat as high as is comfortably possible with your feet remaining firmly planted on the floor.

- If you're petite, avoid letting your feet dangle or resting them on the legs of the chair. It can make you look "smaller" and diminish your presence.

Whether seated or standing, there is a popular pose that accompanies these postures—it is often unconscious and misinterpreted—crossing arms (see Quick Tips).

QUICK TIPS

Crossing Arms

Over the years, a great number of seminar participants have shared that the top two reasons they cross their arms over their chests is for comfort or because they're cold. While understandable, the concern is that others don't always interpret this pose that way. In fact, hundreds over the years have voiced that they're inclined to perceive this as a defensive, unapproachable pose and think the individual is annoyed, disinterested, or standoffish.

In addition, if you're in a leadership role, crossing your arms may also send the signal that you're dissatisfied, upset, or disapproving or make you appear intimidating, which could create a divide with members of your team.

Whichever postures you choose, the key is that you're consciously making a choice that supports how you want to be perceived.

MOVEMENT

On one of my recent trips to Georgia for a speaking engagement, while waiting for my flight, I saw a woman walking by who immediately caught my attention. The way she was shuffling across the floor was so out of place with her poised and elegant demeanor that it reminded me how critical the way we move is to the perception others have of us.

The fourth, and final, element of our physical language is movement.

COACHING CORNER

What are you communicating when you walk?

Do you rush around? Walk slowly and saunter? Move with a confident gait?

It's important to move at a measured pace. This gives the impression that you're confident and focused, and it communicates a calmness that everything is under control. If you're always seen as rushing around, you may be labeled as disorganized, abrupt, or intense. Conversely, if you move too slowly, you may be giving off the impression that you're disinterested, lack initiative, or are slow to get things done. With extremes often come misperceptions—and these characteristics are assumed simply because of how you move.

The key is to move with purpose.

COACHING CORNER

What does your body language communicate?

Have you received feedback on the nonverbal messages you send?

Is there a physical choice you are making that could be undermining you?

Your body language and physical presence send a message well before you speak. It helps others decide how to view your confidence, capability, and professionalism.

YOUR QUESTIONS ANSWERED

Some of the most common nonverbal communication questions I'm asked include:

1. *"I naturally have 'RBF.' What can I do about it?"*

   Some individuals find that others misinterpret their natural, neutral facial expression as annoyance or anger. People who have experienced this misperception, have tagged it "RBF," also known as "resting b*tch face."

   My guidance is to make a conscious effort to smile more, engage in small talk, and have softer eyes. These tweaks will balance out others' misperceptions of you—or any intensity that may be reflected in your face.

2. *"If you're late to a meeting, and don't want to be misperceived as disorganized or chaotic, what do you do?"*

   If you're late to a meeting, run up to the closed door and then walk in calmly, confidently, and quietly. Whether or not you need to apologize for being late will be determined by what you find when you enter the room. If colleagues are waiting for you to start, an apology is required; if they're already engaged in agenda items, simply acknowledging to your host after the fact may do the trick (for more on *apologizing* vs. *acknowledging*, see Chapter 4). Irrespective of that, never appear frazzled or rushed—only calm and composed.

3. *"If you are not a 'smiler,' how can you smile more?"*

   A sincere smile can quickly help to reduce tension, instantly make others feel comfortable around you, and project that you're friendly and approachable. I recommend making a concerted effort to reflect a slight smile when possible, more approachable facial expressions in general, and a friendly demeanor—all of which may coax the smile to come or compensate when you're not smiling.

Great opportunities to flash a sincere smile or reflect an approachable demeanor include when:

- Meeting people

- Introducing yourself

- Entering and exiting a group conversation

- Starting or ending a presentation or participating in the Q&A portion

- Saying positive words, such as "I'm *delighted* to share this *great* news with you."

4. **"In speaking about facial expressions, what are your thoughts around the topic of makeup?"**

Makeup is a great way to accentuate your features, create a polished look, and communicate that you've given thought and care to your overall appearance. Is it a requirement? No. If you're interested in experimenting with different looks, YouTube has some great tutorials from renowned makeup influencers, or the makeup counter at a department store may be a less intimidating starting point.

Besides the personal satisfaction you may get from wearing makeup, research shows there may also be a monetary incentive. The *New York Times* published a study that indicated women who wear makeup earn 20 percent more in their professional lifetime than those who go without.[3]

Now that you've delved deeply into first impressions and perceptions, created an *accurate* impression—the one that *you* want others to have of you—and projected confidence and presence through your body, let's now focus on how you can maintain that perception through your verbal communication.

CHAPTER FOUR

SPEAKING WITH INTENTION

The right word may be effective,
but no word was ever as effective
as a rightly timed pause.

—MARK TWAIN
American humorist, journalist,
lecturer, and novelist

n the last chapter, we explored the first of three main ways we communicate when face-to-face: through nonverbal messaging. In this chapter, we'll focus on the other two ways: through our vocal delivery and words.

If you've ever cringed when listening to someone sabotage his or her own idea or noticed a colleague's overuse of the phrase "Sorry," you've seen the impact that vocal delivery and word choice can have on perception. How you sound and what you say can instantly support or undermine the impression you want to make. Knowing this will serve you well when you're trying to grab the audience's attention, persuade someone to buy into your idea, or be seen as diplomatic and tactful.

COACHING CORNER

Do you communicate confidence and speak with intention?

Circle the answers that best describe you.

1. Do you speak at a measured pace?

   Never   Occasionally   Always

2. Do you use the phrase "I think," "I feel," or "I believe"?

   Never   Occasionally   Always

3. Do you consciously modify your volume to suit the situation, setting, or person?

   Never   Occasionally   Always

4. Do you speak with "uptalk" or "upswing"—a way of speaking reflected by the often unconscious rise in pitch at the end of a statement, making it sound like a question?

   Never   Occasionally   Always

5. Do you over-apologize?

   Never   Occasionally   Always

6. Do you carry the energy through the entire word or phrase so that it's clearly heard?

   Never   Occasionally   Always

7. Do you use "filler words," such as "um," "basically," "like," or "so"?

   Never   Occasionally   Always

8. Do you overexplain?

   Never   Occasionally   Always

9. Do you easily engage your audience?

   Never   Occasionally   Always

Sometimes one aspect of your communication can tend to influence another person's overall impression of your confidence and competence. Therefore, it's also important to have a sense of the verbal perception that others have of you.

COACHING CORNER

How do people perceive the way you communicate?

Circle any phrases that others could use to describe you.

Doesn't sound confident

Has an aggressive tone

Is too emotional

Speaks in a monotone voice

Is too direct

Needs to speak up more

Is too nice

Is quick to react

Speaks very fast

As you review both assessments, take note of your strengths as well as which areas may be undermining you.

This chapter will highlight six vocal delivery elements that can help— or hinder—your communication. It will focus on commonly used words and phrases that may be undermining the impact of your message. It will also address key strategies that can empower you to speak with intention and make a positive impression.

Let's get started.

VOCAL VISIBILITY

Your "vocal visibility," which I also refer to as your "verbal presence," is as important as your visual presence. Six vocal delivery elements have the power to help you instantly communicate confidence, clarity, and diplomacy—or diminish the impact of your message.

1. Pitch

2. Pace

3. Tone

4. Inflection

5. Articulation

6. Volume

Let's define these six vocal delivery elements and the importance of each in greater detail.

1. Pitch—How High or Deep Your Voice Is

Pitch can be strategically used to engage the listener, add a level of light-heartedness, indicate a question, and give credibility and weight to your words.

In business, those who consistently speak in a higher pitch may be taken less seriously than a colleague with a more substantive-sounding voice. The goal is to have a pleasant-sounding pitch. If you would like to change your pitch, it's possible—and you're not alone. Actors, newscasters, and business professionals often work with vocal coaches to change the pitch of their voices to align with the perception they want for themselves or the characters they're playing.

Shifting Your Pitch

If you're unsure what your natural pitch is, one technique is to hum and then speak a few sentences. What you hear, more than likely, will be your natural voice. To shift your pitch, try humming on a lower or higher vocal register—and then speaking in that range.

When it comes to pitch, it's also important to be aware of "uptalk"—also known as "upswing."

Uptalk

This is a vocal habit whereby the speaker changes a statement into a question by ending the sentence on a higher pitch. If the sentence is not supposed to be a question, this can devalue the importance and impact of your words—because it can appear that you're questioning the very message you're trying to convey.

This habit can often manifest unconsciously from feelings of nervousness, insecurity, or uncertainty. Uptalk can be especially undermining when trying to establish credibility, pitching an idea, or having a difficult conversation, such as when negotiating compensation. If done too often, this habit can also become annoying, causing listeners to become distracted from and disinterested in what you're saying.

The key is that your pitch supports and conveys your intended message.

2. Pace—How Fast or Slowly You Speak

Pace can be used strategically to engage, energize, emphasize key information, and maintain the flow and comprehension of what you're saying. It's also heavily influenced by geographical region and profession.

Gauging Your Pace

The average individual speaks between 125 and 150 words per minute. To help gauge your "speech signature"—your natural pace, take a look at the guidelines below:

- Slow: less than 110 words per minute

- Conversational: 120–150 words per minute

- Fast: more than 160 words per minute

In comparison, radio hosts speak between 150 and 160 words per minute and auctioneers and sports commentators speak between 250 and 400 words per minute.[1]

Speaking at a faster pace can reflect confidence, knowledge, passion, and credibility. It can also make you appear nervous, uncomfortable, or arrogant. It can unconsciously communicate that your message isn't worth the listener's time—and even that you don't want to be there. Individuals who speak very quickly may also sound as if they're mumbling because words lose their clarity, sentences start to run together, phrases start to drop, and the ends of words trail off. Depending on the complexity of the information, speaking too fast could result in your content losing value and your delivery sounding monotone or condescending.

Conversely, speaking at a slower pace can reflect thoughtfulness, sincerity, empathy, and trustworthiness. It can also cause listeners to quickly lose interest or question your confidence. They may even doubt the validity of what you're saying if it becomes too difficult to follow the flow—and, therefore, comprehend your message.

Ideally, your delivery will include strategically using pace—since variety gives life to what you're saying and can increase engagement.

The key is to speak at a measured pace and according to both your audience and your end goals.

Shifting Your Pace

Strategically adding pauses, and knowing how to increase or decrease your pace, can add impact.

Pausing

There are two types of pauses—active and passive.

A "passive pause" is often unintentional and is the by-product of uncertainty. It happens when you stop talking and appear to be "searching" for what to say next. You may experience a passive pause if you've lost your train of thought, aren't sure what to say, or nerves have gotten the better of you.

An "active pause" is when you *intentionally* stop talking. It's done for a specific purpose, such as to smile at or connect with the audience, emphasize a key concept, or allow listeners to feel the impact of what you've said. Active pauses are strategically placed to add engagement and reflect that you're in control of the content and your delivery of it.

If you don't pause, you may be perceived as monopolizing a conversation, reciting a monologue, or as an incessant lecturer. You're also forcing the audience to internalize content without allowing them time to process it, which can be overwhelming and exhausting for many. People process information at different rates, so pausing will allow you to accommodate diverse listening and learning styles.

Decreasing Your Pace

One way to naturally slow your pace is by practicing what you want to say. Feeling confident with your content will also help you to have more command over your message. Being comfortably confident with the words you say can combat nervousness and help you keep from speeding up your speech—which is often the natural reflex of the body when you're public-facing and in nerve-racking situations.

Increasing Your Pace

A strategy to naturally increase your pace, and the flow of your words, is to eliminate "filler words" from your speech. Adding irrelevant words takes up time, slows down sentences, and detracts and distracts from the concept. Also, avoid pausing after every few words and instead pause strategically.

3. Tone—the Mood or Emotion
Behind Your Words

Tone is the vocal delivery element that's most often misinterpreted. It represents a broad range of emotion and can instantly indicate how the speaker truly feels. Some individuals are intentional and purposeful about their choice of tone. Many are capable of "masking" their real feelings when they speak, while others unconsciously reveal inner thoughts and feelings through their delivery.

When someone refers or responds unfavorably to *"your tone,"* the emotion they most often hear is some shade of anger. This may or may not be your intention. You may be intently focused, speak in a concise manner, talk at a fast pace, or be a person who doesn't naturally smile. Each action could immediately cause your tone to be misinterpreted as sounding abrupt, hostile, annoyed, defensive, or condescending. If you've received comments about your tone, people may avoid you, fear you, or label you as aggressive, disrespectful, unapproachable, or antagonistic. Therefore, try to ensure that your tone is approachable unless you intentionally make the decision to be perceived otherwise.

If you're commenting to someone about his or her tone, it's important to define what emotion you're hearing. Doing so results in increasing this individual's understanding of what was unsettling to you and how he or she could adjust the delivery, if interested.

4. Inflection—Having Vocal Variety

I define inflection as vocal variety in the voice. It's created by strategically changing your pitch and tone as well as using the elements of pace and volume to help you *sound* interesting. Sometimes you speak faster to keep attention, slow down to emphasize a point, project to be easily heard, or speak with an upbeat tone to grab attention. Inflection can create interest in both the speaker *and* the content, resulting in greater impact.

If you would like to speak with more inflection in your voice, try the following strategies:

- **Think of your voice hooked up to a heart rate monitor.** When you're alive and thriving, your heartbeat is reflected in peaks and valleys of "life." This image of variability can also pertain to when you're speaking with inflection. Adding variability to your voice helps you to sound interesting.

- **Emphasize key words.** Emphasizing certain words usually causes a change in pitch, which helps you to avoid sounding flat.

- **Remember your voice is an instrument.** Your voice can be adjusted to produce the sound you want.

The other side of the heart rate monitor is when you have flatlined—or are using a flat-sounding voice. Having little to no variety in the voice can cause what you say to sound monotone and can be death to a speaker, if your goal is to engage others.

QUICK TIP

Monotone

While inflection can quickly engage your audience, a lack of inflection—or little to no interest in the voice, can result in you sounding monotone. A flat-sounding, boring, or robotic voice will quickly undermine your influencing power, as well as your ability to inspire and keep the audience's attention. Unless it's a strategic choice, avoid speaking in a monotone voice.

The key is that you're only as interesting
as you are interested.

5. Articulation—How Clearly You Speak

A client recently asked me to coach his high school–age son to speak more clearly. Ahead of the son's college interviews, he wanted him to learn how to project the right impression.

"Save your money," I said with a smile. *"Simply ask him to smile more."* My client looked quizzically at me. I continued, *"When the lips are tight, there is less room for the words to get out. Smiling opens up the space for words to flow more freely, which often results in improved articulation."* In addition, when you focus on slowing down your pace, words have more time to be formed—which helps them to sound clearer.

If you want to practice your articulation, a few other techniques to try include:

- **Read an article out loud and emphasize each word.** This overexaggerated way of speaking can help you to speak slower because you're consciously aware of saying each word. The feeling associated with this action can eventually become ingrained, thereby forming a new habit.

- **Record yourself speaking.** This technique allows you to hear exactly what others hear when you're talking. When playing back the recording, listen for instances during which your speech becomes unclear—or it sounds as if you're mumbling. Practice making adjustments.

- **Practice reciting tongue twisters.** This exercise will force you to slow down your speech in order to articulate the difficult rhyming words and alliteration.

Within the category of articulation, there are two significant elements that can help you to reflect polish and professionalism—enunciation and pronunciation.

Enunciation

Enunciation is making sure to say the ends of the words. Carrying the energy through the ends of the words increases speaker clarity, enhances listener comprehension, and establishes a higher degree of "vocal visibility." In order to emphasize your enunciation, practice saying *p*, *t*, *d*, *k*, and many of the end-of-words consonants.

The "trailing off" of words occurs because the energy is not carried through to the end of the word or sentence. This makes it much more difficult for listeners to hear what you're saying. A few ways to address this are by concentrating on keeping your volume continuous, breathing from the diaphragm so that you have enough breath support to finish the sentence with ease, and visualizing someone in the back of the room effortlessly hearing the last few words of each sentence that you say.

Pronunciation

The second element related to articulation is pronunciation—saying the word correctly. If you're not saying the word correctly, for many listening it undermines the perception of your education, knowledge, and ability.

6. Volume—How Loudly or Softly You Speak

I've noticed, experienced, and been guilty of (kudos to sisters for keeping us in check) an outgrowth of the smartphone age—the "loud talker phenomenon." For some reason, individuals will often speak even louder when talking on their phones—which, due to the accessibility of where and when we take phone calls, is not always appropriate or comfortable for others.

A common perception of loud talkers is that they lack self-awareness, and for soft talkers it's that they don't believe what they have to say is important. Strategically decided, the volume of your voice has significant power when it comes to perception.

If you're trying to remind someone to speak with more volume, avoid asking this individual to "speak louder." Louder is not always appropriate and can often make a shy or quiet person feel uncomfortable. Instead ask him or her to use a "stronger voice" or to "project more." You might say . . .

> "I want to hear what you have to say. Could you please use a stronger voice."

> "So that everyone can hear you could you project a little more."

There are two techniques that work very well if *you* are trying to speak with more volume.

Technique #1: Speak from the Diaphragm—instead of the chest or nose. By taking deep breaths into the diaphragm you'll have greater breath support, which can give you a stronger-sounding voice. Conversely, breathing from the chest is often too shallow and results in your sounding breathy; while breathing from the nose keeps the breath in a small space, often resulting in a higher pitch.

Technique #2: Stand up when you speak whenever possible and appropriate. By standing you elongate your core, allowing more breath into your diaphragm, which allows you to more easily support and project your voice.

Be courteous to those around you by being mindful of how loudly you're speaking and for how long—especially in an open seating plan or shared space. Without even realizing it, your volume can also increase when you're passionate or excited. Speaking with enthusiasm or energy is important to your being engaging. These good intentions can be easily misinterpreted if someone doesn't share your energy or like your volume. Instead you could be perceived as emotional, pushy, yelling—and, depending on your tone, aggressive.

If you naturally have an enthusiastic, outgoing, loud-volume voice, think of your voice as a dimmer-style light switch—or the speedometer in a car: 100 percent may be too much, and you have to dim or reduce your volume to 70 percent for some and 40 percent for others.

The key is to be aware of your volume so you can effectively communicate your message and support the perception you want others to have of you.

Sometimes one aspect will undermine the perception you want to project. More often, there's a compounding effect. An individual who speaks fast paired with her soft-volume voice could be viewed as nervous and lacking confidence. An individual who has an abrupt tone and speaks loudly may be misperceived as aggressive, domineering, demanding, or a bully. A professional who comes home still in the mindset of work could unconsciously speak in a "business tone," making her loved ones feel she is distant or annoyed.

COACHING CORNER

Which of the vocal delivery elements have you mastered?

What about your vocal delivery could be acting as a barrier when you communicate?

Being aware of *how* you sound and mastering these six vocal delivery elements will allow you to communicate your message effectively and support the perception you want others to have of you—so, too, will your words.

. . .

Speaking to thousands of professionals across the country each year has given me the opportunity to hear their stories, answer their questions, and help them to navigate workplace conversations and situations. I've come to realize the extent to which certain words and phrases can either advance or stifle the importance of what someone is saying. The words we choose are the third and final way in which we communicate.

COACHING CORNER

Do you use certain words because it helps to soften your message or you're afraid to sound like a know-it-all?

UNDERMINING WORDS

Your choice of words can empower what you're saying or weaken the meaning of your message. Verbally, or in writing, if your words are wishy-washy or weak, it may undermine the urgency or importance of your message. If someone can't get passed the "filler words"—meaningless words such as "um," "you know"—that you're saying, the listener may become so distracted that he or she does not hear the core message that you're saying.

Here are some of the words and phrases you may want to avoid using in a professional setting:

- **Superficial language,** which is used to make you seem closer to someone than you actually are (*"My man, how goes it?" or "She'll be right with you, love."*).

- **Lazy language,** which gained its name from the speaker dropping the ends of words ("gonna," "wanna").

- **Slang,** which in many work environments can represent a lack of sophistication and professionalism (text lingo in emails or extremely casual language).

- **Inappropriate or derogatory words and humor,** which is considered anything that *other people* may find offensive—even if you don't. If there's even the slightest chance your words or humor could be misinterpreted, refrain.

- **Word inflation** describes a word or phrase that is said so frequently that it becomes overused to the point of annoyance (*Let's put that in the parking lot*).

- **Overusing jargon and industry- or position-specific terms** is word inflation specific to your work environment and industry.

- **Negativity and gossip** creating or fostering drama will never serve you well or invite the perception you want others to form of you; refrain.

- **Mispronounced words** can quickly undermine your credibility ("irregardless" instead of "regardless" or "conversate" instead of "conversation" or "converse")

- **Young language** could create the feeling that you are younger or less experienced than you are ("totally," "my bad," "Gucci" = good, "woke" = awareness).

There are also words and phrases whose power to undermine you may not be as obvious. They fall into the following categories:

Over-Apologizing	Weak
Fillers	Erasers
Self-Sabotaging	Charged

Let's explore each of these undermining word categories in greater detail.

Over-Apologizing

Are you a self-proclaimed "sorry sayer"—constantly saying you're sorry? Or do you get annoyed because you always hear someone else saying it when he or she has done nothing wrong? If so, you're experiencing the trap of over-apologizing.

Some cultures say sorry for various reasons and view the meaning and the frequency differently. In England and Japan frequently saying sorry is generally appreciated, as the British consider it courteous and the Japanese see it as showing deference. In contrast, in many professional arenas across the United States, constantly saying sorry has become an unconscious knee-jerk response or is intentionally used to "soften" a sentiment—and can be perceived as weak.

"Over the next um—sorry—20 minutes . . ."

"Hey Grace, sorry, can I get a few minutes . . ."

"Sorry, I have a question . . ."

According to research, the word "sorry" can be traced back to the Old English word *sarig*, which means "distressed, grieved, or full of sorrow."[2] Following that translation, we would use the word "sorry" only when we had made a mistake and needed to rectify it. Instead today, the word "sorry" has morphed into meaning *"excuse me," "my fault," "I'm uncomfortable,"* and *"I'm not sure what to say."* It has also become an automatic response, as the speaker tries to regain his or her thought or composure.

With the word "sorry" so frequently said, especially in business, the meaning behind the word has become hollow and meaningless for many—especially when an apology *is* required. In light of the word "sorry" becoming a filler word, let's highlight how you can make sure to deliver a meaningful apology:

- **Use *"I apologize"* vs. *"I'm sorry."*** Because the word "sorry" has become so overly used, the phrase "I apologize" may carry more meaning and sound more impactful.

- **Apologize in person.** Standing in front of someone and taking responsibility for a behavior or action can be nerve-racking. It can also be incredibly rewarding because there's a good chance the apology will salvage the rapport—and expedite the process of recovering, rebuilding, and reestablishing. In-person interactions have healing properties that other communication mediums don't share because they combine three powerful cues: body, voice, and words. Together, these three cues send a more impactful message to the recipient.

  If you can't apologize face-to-face, then do so over the phone. If you can't apologize voice-to-voice, then wait. The impact of your apology over email becomes diluted since the recipient can't see your body language or hear your delivery.

- **Apologize to people individually.** If you need to apologize to more than one person, approach each person separately. It sends a different message and may dilute the impact of your gesture, if you clump everyone together. Just as you might send individual thank you notes after an interview if more than one person interviewed you, apologizing to people separately demonstrates that you recognize the impact your action may have had on each person.

If there are situations where you need to apologize to a group of people or to one individual in front of others, make the apology as personal as possible. You can achieve this by making eye contact with, and speaking to, each recipient of the apology.

- **Eliminate "expiration date" mentality.** If you decide an apology is required, it means that something significant has happened that needs to be addressed or rectified. If, for whatever reason, you were unable to apologize—or chose not to—and now time has passed, it's never too late. Even if roles have changed, it feels awkward, you're embarrassed, or you wonder if the other person even still cares (most likely they do)—apologies are like thank you notes: they don't have an expiration date.

  There are instances in which the recipient has moved on from the incident, you don't want to rehash it, or your instinct is not to address the situation. If this is the case, trust your judgment. As long as you've made a conscious decision and have specific reasons to support your decision, then you know you're erring on the side of doing what's right versus defaulting to what's easy.

- **Avoid oversaturation.** If your apology is sincere, there is no reason to keep apologizing for the same mistake. That action will make you look weak, may encourage others to take advantage of your vulnerability, and is annoying to many.

- **Consider delivery.** The words you choose, in conjunction with your nonverbal and vocal delivery, will make your apology meaningful.

When you do need to apologize, use the three key steps of the following Apology Template to deliver a meaningful one. Using the Apology Template will help the recipient of your apology to see that you gave the situation a lot of consideration and are holding yourself accountable—which shows that you're respectful, considerate, and self-aware.

Apology Template

Let's suppose you had to present in this week's senior staff meeting with two of your team members. It turns out you got stuck in traffic and missed the meeting, which negatively impacted your team members because they missed an opportunity to present their work—and shine in front of senior leadership. Senior leadership may have also misinterpreted your absence as a reflection of your team's overall credibility. Therefore, an apology is due.

- **Step 1: Personalize.** Use the person's name, state your apology, and be specific regarding why you're apologizing in a sentence or two. Avoid giving excuses.

  "Alli, I'd like to apologize for missing this morning's meeting with senior staff."

- **Step 2: Rectify.** State how you will *immediately* rectify the situation, if possible. *Immediately* is the key word, which is reflected by two elements—action and time.

  "Within the next 45 minutes, I'll email each person who was at the meeting with the research that I would have presented."

  Sometimes rectifying the situation is not possible. When this is the case, it's important to apologize—and then acknowledge this fact. It shows you're aware of the significance of the situation and have the confidence, maturity, and professionalism to address a tough conversation and potentially awkward outcome.

  "Alli, I'd like to apologize for missing this morning's meeting with senior staff. I want you to know that I recognize that missing the meeting was far from ideal since senior leadership was only in New York for the day."

- **Step 3: Prevent.** State how you will prevent this same mistake from recurring and be specific. Avoid giving excuses, which can frustrate the recipient and dilute your message. Simply state the facts. In addition, following through on what you commit to is essential—or your credibility and trustworthiness will be in question.

> *"Going forward, I'll take public transportation to avoid rush hour traffic and I'll arrive to our next two meetings 30 minutes early."*

Full Apology

Here's the full apology in action:

> *"Alli, I'd like to apologize for missing this morning's meeting with senior staff. Within the next 45 minutes, I'll email each person who was at the meeting with the research that I would have presented. Going forward, I'll take public transportation to avoid rush hour traffic and I'll arrive to our next two meetings 30 minutes early."*

- **Optional—Step 4: Check.** After apologizing, depending on the context, severity, and person(s) involved, you may want to include a fourth step.

  It may be important for you to know where you stand with the recipient of your apology. This more than likely can be achieved by laying out the apology as detailed above—and then asking, *"Are we okay?"* or *"Does that sound fair?"* By asking the question, you may find out that your plan to rectify and prevent was not enough, or that the person is too offended to forgive. The knowledge gained will help you to interpret, as well as could influence, your future interactions with this individual.

The key is that your approach allows you to smooth things over enough to maintain the rapport or enables you both to move on.

There's an important distinction to make—the difference between "apologizing" and "acknowledging." Both are extremely meaningful when used accurately. A good rule of thumb is that an apology is required when you have negatively impacted another—most other interactions can be acknowledged.

Acknowledging

The act of acknowledging shows that you're aware of the significance of a situation and have the confidence, maturity, initiative, and professionalism to take ownership of your actions—even when a formal apology is not required.

Let's take a closer look at some scenarios that may require an acknowledgment or apology:

Scenario 1: Late to a Meeting

If you're late arriving to a meeting and your colleagues waited for you to start, then an apology to the group is in order for being late. If you don't apologize, you run the risk of indirectly communicating to your colleagues that their time is less valuable than yours.

One way to approach the apology is this:

> *"I apologize for being late; my previous meeting ran over. Thank you for waiting."*

If your colleagues did *not* wait for you to arrive, then after the meeting concludes, it's important to acknowledge your lateness to whoever is leading the meeting. Your acknowledgment will show a high level of professionalism and communicate to this individual that you respect him or her. The person may, in turn, give some show of appreciation to you for making mention of the situation.

> *"Joan, I want to acknowledge that I was late because my previous meeting ran over. Next time I'll try to leave the prior meeting a few minutes earlier."*

The most important aspect of apologizing or acknowledging is that you're comfortable with the words you're saying. This way you sound natural, heartfelt, and sincere. If the word "acknowledge" is not a word that you would naturally say, try using it. Sometimes in getting out of your comfort zone and practicing something new, you create optionality and foster self-growth. There's also another word you can try using: "recognize."

> *"Joan, I want to recognize that I was late arriving to your meeting. My previous meeting ran over."*

I've been asked by some of the professionals with whom we coach, if they can replace the words "acknowledge" and "recognize" with the word "realize."

> *"Joan, I realize that I was late to your meeting. My previous meeting ran over."*

The accountability factor, which is a critical element in the resolution process, is diminished. The phrase *"I realize . . ."* doesn't reflect the same innate awareness or regard as does *"I want to recognize . . ."* Instead the phrase *"I realize . . ."* leaves me thinking, *so you realize; and what are you going to do about it?* This phrase is more self-focused and not other-focused—which is what you want an apology or acknowledgment to be.

Scenario 2: Ownership of Others' Mistakes

If you manage a team and someone on your team makes a mistake, it's not an immediate cue for you to apologize—*you* didn't make the mistake.

The key is to take ownership for the slip-ups that you directly make.

If you take on others' oversights, you may become the person people start to dump on. Instead, it's much more important and beneficial for you to *lead through the mistake* and stop the hemorrhaging. Focus on acknowledging the faux pas and immediately trying to rectify the situation. This may entail thinking outside of the box, going above and beyond, or asking how you can make it better.

"Anwar, I was told that we dropped the ball on making sure your phone calls to us were returned in a timely manner. This is not the customer service we are known for offering. What can we do to rectify this situation for you?"

The example reflects *". . . **we** dropped the ball."* No need to throw anyone under the bus unless extraordinary circumstances exist. Names may have to be brought up internally so that behaviors are addressed, people are held accountable, and the incident can be documented. You can hold your team member accountable internally while externally showing a unified front. This approach also demonstrates that your priorities are the client and resolving the mistake as quickly as possible—not placing blame.

Depending on the particular players involved, the specific situation, and the mistake that was made, there may be instances where you feel it *is* in your best interest to apologize for someone's mistake. The differentiating factor is that you're making the deliberate decision to do so—and not just defaulting to the action out of habit.

Scenario 3: Expressing Condolences

If you want to express empathy or condolences, instead of saying *"I'm sorry for your loss"* (because you've now decided to reserve the word "sorry" for when you've made a mistake and negatively impacted another), try one of the following:

- *"We're thinking of you during this difficult time."*

- *"I can't imagine what you're going through."*

- *"My heart goes out to you."*

- *"Our thoughts and prayers are with you."*

- *"Please accept my deepest sympathy for your loss."*

- *"I want to express my condolences to you and your family."*

If you *are* at fault and want the other person to know that you're acutely aware of how you have negatively impacted him or her, your goal is to apologize or acknowledge with empathy.

Apologizing and Acknowledging with Empathy

An empathic apology could be worded as:

> "I see that you're <u>angry</u> (emotion said by speaker) *because of*
> <u>my correcting you in front of our team and senior leadership—</u>
> (key message shared by speaker). *That would upset me as well.*
> *I apologize. Here are my thoughts about what I can do differently*
> *going forward . . ."*

If the situation doesn't warrant an apology and you feel something needs to be said, an empathic acknowledgment of the situation may be the key:

> "I can see you are _____ (insert emotion said by speaker)
> *because of* _____ (add key message shared by speaker).
> *I want you to know that was not my intention."*

COACHING CORNER

Is there someone to whom you owe an apology or acknowledgment?

Considering the important elements shared, what will it now sound like?

Weak Words

Weak words can immediately minimize the impact and value of what you're saying, thereby undermining your confidence and competence in the eyes of others.

Three widely used weak phrases are:

"I Think"

- "I think we should reduce the number of monthly team meetings."

- "Some of my strengths, I think, are . . ."

"I Believe"

- *"I believe this gives us an opportunity to shine in front of the client."*

- *"The numbers on the report speak for themselves, I believe."*

"I Feel"

- *"I feel like dress down Fridays is the way to go."*

- *"It would be a mistake, I feel, not to move forward on this."*

There may be specific industries or instances when using these words is required and appreciated.

The key is to be intentional about your choice of words— and where and when you use them.

Utilizing weak words can quickly create doubt, uncertainty, or make what you say sound wishy-washy. When guiding individuals to abandon using weak words so that they sound more confident, competent, and create impact when they speak, two of the biggest responses I hear are:

"I don't want it to seem like I definitely have the answer or am being pushy."

"I'm trying to soften what I'm saying."

I understand.

It can feel like a major risk, if we don't hedge our core message with a "weak word" and then it's not well received. Part of addressing this concern is to adjust your vocal delivery, which can quickly help to curb the fear of sounding pushy or arrogant. Your vocal delivery and how you communicate the intention and meaning behind your words, in partnership with the actual words that you choose, set the tone. Since we have already highlighted the importance of vocal delivery in conveying your message, let's focus on word choice.

To avoid lessening the value of what you say, replace weak words with more substantive words. Substantive words have natural weight to them; they innately reflect commitment, show thought, add value, and don't underestimate the belief in one's own idea. Some of my favorite words that maintain the balance between strength and humility, and could replace "I think," "I believe," and "I feel" are:

- Thought: *"My thought on that is . . ."*

- Idea: *"Based on the research, my idea is to . . ."*

- Recommendation: *"After hearing all of the information, my recommendation would be to . . ."*

- Suggestion: *"Here's my suggestion . . ."*

- Guidance: *"Based on what everyone has said, my guidance is . . ."*

- Perspective: *"My perspective on that is . . ."*

As you consider replacing weak words with more substantive alternatives, compare the following responses and the perceptions that may result.

Using Weak Words Perception: Uncertainty	Omitting Weak Words Possible Perception: Definitive or Pushy	Substituting Weak Words Intended Perception: Strength and Humility
"I think we should reduce the number of monthly team meetings."	*"We should reduce the number of monthly team meetings."*	*"My idea is we reduce the number of monthly team meetings."* *"My guidance is we reduce the number of monthly team meetings."*
"I believe this gives us an opportunity to shine in front of the client."	*"This gives us an opportunity to shine in front of the client."*	*"My thought is this gives us an opportunity to shine in front of the client."* *"My perspective is that we want every opportunity to shine in front of the client."*

Using Weak Words Perception: Uncertainty	Omitting Weak Words Possible Perception: Definitive or Pushy	Substituting Weak Words Intended Perception: Strength and Humility
"I feel it would be a mistake not to move forward on this."	*"It would be a mistake not to move forward on this."*	*"My idea is that we move forward on this."* *"My recommendation is moving forward on this is the way to go."*

COACHING CORNER

Which word do you find yourself using most?

"I think"   "I believe"   "I feel"

If you were going to substitute it, which substantive word would you go with?

Thought   Idea   Recommendation

Suggestion   Guidance   Perspective

There are other weak words and phrases that you may be *unconsciously* using: *just, possibly, I hope, I suppose, I guess, kinda,* and *maybe*.

To prevent unintentionally creating doubt or uncertainty around what you're saying, focus on simply omitting these words or phrases or finding ways to rephrase. For example:

- *"Can I ~~just~~ get five minutes of your time?"*

- *"Here's another idea that might work ~~maybe~~."*

- *"Could we ~~possibly~~ meet to go over these numbers in greater detail?"*

- "~~I suppose~~ the way we could handle this is to call the vendor."

- "I ~~just~~ have one question."

- "~~I guess~~ this is a very important client."

- "There is really no other option, ~~I suppose~~."

- Weak: "~~I hope~~ (Direct) I explained that well."

    Rephrase: "Did I answer your question?"

    Rephrase: "What clarification can I give?"

COACHING CORNER

What are some phrases that you catch yourself saying that may be undermining you in the eyes of others?

Knowing what you now know, how would you change those phrases to be more substantive?

Potentially undermining phrases:

More substantive:

Filler Words

Another cluster of words that speakers frequently say, without even realizing it, fall under the category of "filler words," which are also referred to as "nervous language" and "speech clutter." Filler words are meaningless words that can make you sound nervous or uncertain and confuse the clarity of your message. They take up valuable airtime because they don't help to progress the idea forward and they can detract from both communicating and comprehending the core message. In fact, the consistent use of these tiny words can overshadow the competence of the speaker—even without him or her being aware.

Some well-known and also not-so-obvious filler words include:

- Um

- Uh

- Like

- So

- You know / Ya know

- Basically

- Actually

- Definitely

- Obviously

- Okay

- Literally

- Ultimately

- Essentially

- Yeah

- Well

- And (elongated or exaggerated)

- Right (habitually placed within or at the end of a sentence even though it's not reflecting a question)

    "I know it's delicious, right."

    "It's a good one, right, and that's why we . . ."

COACHING CORNER

Do you use filler words?

If so, which one(s) do you use most often?

The use of one or two filler words in conversation and during a presentation is fine. We're human, and we're not always going to speak perfectly. In fact, this book is not about making you a perfect communicator—it's about helping you to be an *effective* communicator.

The focus of this section is to break the habit of allowing filler words to creep into your communication—and the use of filler words *is*, in fact, a verbal habit. Similar to most habits, it's hard to break. The good news is this habit *can* be broken.

Some techniques to reduce and eliminate filler words include:

- **Look for any filler words that you include in emails and remove them.** Recognizing the use of filler words visually may help you to become more aware of them verbally.

- **Avoid making your first word a filler word.** As you practice reducing and eliminating filler words, start with a quick and easy goal—that the first word you say can't be a filler word. Research reflects that the average adult attention span is approximately five minutes.[3] During this time, listeners are making the determination if they want to continue listening—engage them with what you say.

- **Listen for others using filler words.** If you can recognize when others use speech clutter, you may be more apt to hear it when you speak. Awareness of others is power and the impetus for self-change.

- **Be aware if you use filler words during personal conversations.** If you're using filler words with friends and family—when you're most comfortable—you're more than likely using them in your work world where the comfort level can be less.

- **Start to recognize when and where you use filler words at work.** Sometimes filler words are used more often in nerve-racking and uncomfortable situations or with specific or intimidating people. If this is the case, make more of an effort to rehearse what you want to say for these particular circumstances. When you feel comfortable speaking, you're less apt to use this "nervous language."

- **Practice what you want to say.** Many people think faster than they speak. With the brain trying to organize your thoughts and reflect them through your words live-time, "nervous language" may unconsciously creep in because your words can't be formulated fast enough. Thinking about and practicing what you want to say will help to reduce this undermining tendency.

- **Pause.** When you're not sure what you want to say, take an "active pause"—a few seconds to breathe, smile, or turn the attention onto the audience. This will allow you to gather your thoughts, thereby reducing the chance of "speech clutter." It's more impactful to pause and think about what you want to say than to keep talking and use "nervous language."

- **Have an accountability partner.** An accountability partner is someone who can help you to gauge how you're doing with a predetermined goal. Be careful who you choose to take on this role— think about someone you trust, who will hold your confidence, has your best interests in mind, and can help you to change the desired behavior. Ask this person to share when he or she hears you using filler words. Give guidelines for how you want to be told (in the moment or after the fact), and in which situations, or around which people, you would feel comfortable being corrected. In general, it's most helpful to understand which filler words you use, and when you use them, by being told in the moment.

- **Record yourself.** Before a meeting or presentation, use your smartphone to practice and record your delivery. Listening to yourself can start increasing your awareness to any nervous language, or other verbal habits, that could be undermining you or annoying to the listener.

Eraser Words

Think pencil eraser. "Eraser words" "erase" or eliminate anything positive or important that came before them. Example eraser words include:

- But

- However

- Yet

- Despite

- On the other hand

- Although

- That (being) said . . .

- Nevertheless

- Otherwise

Most people don't realize that they've inserted an eraser word into the sentence, thereby changing the meaning.

"I have an idea; however, it might not work."

"I agree with you; that said, we have a couple of options."

You want your words to have weight—your sentiments to be meaningful. If you use eraser words, you may find that the various elements of your message are not heard with equal impact. Removing eraser words allows each sentiment to have its own importance and be heard. This becomes tremendously important when suggesting an idea to leadership or preparing for any important meeting or presentation—and you want to be heard and have your words matter.

This concept is equally essential when it comes to giving performance evaluations or sharing feedback.

Eraser Words and Feedback

Research shows that a top reason why employees leave their jobs is lack of recognition. A new study from the global employee engagement company Reward Gateway shows that of 5,812 employees surveyed across the United Kingdom, United States, and Australia, 69 percent felt demotivated by a lack of recognition.[4]

Leaders often respond that they *are* giving praise, while many employees say they don't get recognition—this disconnect may be the unconscious insertion of eraser words when delivering feedback.

> *"Fred, great job finishing that client proposal by deadline <u>but</u> let's talk about how we can save even more time as we approach it going forward."*

The word "but" in the sentence erased the positive feedback given to Fred. Instead, Fred more than likely heard that he needs to do something differently going forward. He may even interpret the feedback with annoyance, wondering why he's not being recognized for a job well done.

The key is to make the feedback into two separate sentences.

There needs to be a balance: wanting the individual to hear the positive feedback or praise and also honoring that additional direction or thoughts need to be shared. Eliminate the eraser word "but" from the feedback and convert the feedback into two separate sentences. This way, Fred gets to enjoy the positive feedback, and he also hears about the opportunities for improvement.

> *"Fred, great job finishing that client proposal by deadline. Let's talk about how we can save even more time as we approach it going forward."*

Using the Word "And"

I'm often asked if using the word "and" to connect the two thoughts is an appropriate alternative to making the feedback two separate sentences.

"Fred, great job finishing that client proposal by deadline, and I'd also like to talk about how we can save even more time as we approach it going forward."

On the pro side, the word "and" is more positive than using an eraser word. On the con side, the whole purpose of the word "and" is to connect thoughts. When thoughts are connected, sometimes the brain combines them. As a result, the listener gets to use his or her discretion as to what's heard or given weight. When you're trying to balance giving praise with developmental feedback, you want the sentiments to have the same weight and impact. Using the word "and" may end up combining the thoughts and lessening the importance of one over the other.

The next time you need to make an important point, give feedback, or share a thought either in conversation or over email, consciously decide to eliminate eraser words—and see if you notice a difference in the recipient's response.

Self-Sabotaging Words

Sometimes when a situation makes you uncomfortable or a person makes you nervous, you doubt yourself. When those feelings of discomfort, nervousness, or doubt are reflected in what you say, you can appear to undermine or sabotage yourself. Do not be the driver of the bus that runs you over!

Phrases that can act as self-sabotaging mechanisms to your competence, confidence, and credibility include:

- *"Bear with me, I'm not the authority on this."*

- *"Don't quote me."*

- *"What do I know . . ."*

- *"I'm no expert, but . . ."*

- *"But I digress."*

- *"It could just be me."*

- *"In my (humble) opinion . . ."*

- *"Can I be honest?" | "To be honest."*

- *"With all due respect . . ."*

- *"Here's what I think . . . is that right?"*

- *"I hope that's okay."*

- *"We've done it this way for 20 years."*

- *"I know I look young."*

- A dead-end *"I don't know"* or *"No."*

- *"This may be wrong, but . . ."*

- *"Correct me if I'm wrong . . ."*

- *"This may be a stupid question . . ."*

- *"This might not be such a great idea, but . . ."*

- *"You may have already said this . . ."*

- *"I know you're busy, but . . .*

- *"I don't want to interrupt, but . . ."*

Some other phrases require both an explanation and an alternative. Let's work through those now:

- *"I hate to bother you . . ."*
  The speaker is trying to show respect by acknowledging that the individual is busy. In reality, the exact opposite messaging is being communicated. With the inclusion of the "eraser word" "but," the message is *"I know you're busy and that doesn't really matter so I'm still going to bother you."* In addition, without a valid reason for why the speaker is approaching this busy individual, the recipient may be thinking, *"Well, if you know you're bothering me, why are you?"*

You have two options in this case to show consideration that this person is busy. You could say:

"I have a time-sensitive matter. Do you have a minute?"

This communicates the urgency of *why* you are approaching this person when you know he or she is busy. Or:

"I know you're busy. Do you have five minutes so I can keep the ball rolling on this?"

This communicates progress, which most people don't want to delay or impede, and creates a valid reason for why you're approaching the person. Be mindful that this person may not be able to speak with you in the moment. If that happens, suggest another time.

- *"Can I ask a question?"*
  There's no need to ask for permission; simply ask your question. If you're using the phrase as a way of getting attention, or creating a break in the conversation so that you can ask your question, try the following techniques instead:

  - Lean forward and in the direction of the speaker—shifting your body language into more of an "active" or involved posture can often signal to others that you have something to say.

  - Make eye contact with the speaker.

  - Reflect through your facial expressions that you have a question or would like to interject.

  - Say the speaker's name *first* to create a natural pause in the conversation and then add your thoughts.

  - Find something being said that you can use as a transition statement to continue with what you want to say.

  - Apply the "Bridge Technique" (more on this in Chapter 5).

- *"I don't understand."*

  It's absolutely fair not to understand something. Depending on the situation and people involved, you may not want to phrase a quest for clarification in those words. It may reflect poorly on your ability or knowledge base, especially if others feel you should, as part of your role, be able to understand.

  Alternative statements that capture the meaning behind this phrase without the undermining aspect include:

  "Can you say more about that?"

  "Would you share more about what you mean?"

  "Could you give more details around . . ."

Self-sabotaging phrases don't add weight, value, or impact to what you're saying. In some cases, they do the exact opposite—they give your cheat sheet of insecurities to others and frame what you're saying with uncertainty and doubt.

QUICK TIP

Overusing Jargon

Another way professionals self-sabotage is by overusing jargon. Overusing internal company jargon, industry-specific verbiage, or technical terms can make you sound intimidating, arrogant, and condescending to others. The goal is for you to communicate confidence and instill belief in your competence and ability without making others feel "less-than."

Charged Words

Our last category of undermining words and phrases is "charged words." Similar to the other words and phrases in this chapter, charged words, which I also refer to as "finger-pointing" words, have the power to undermine the perception you want others to have of you.

Depending on the environment, the specific situation, the context surrounding the communication, and the person with whom you're speaking, when spoken alone these words have impact. When paired together, and in conjunction with the vocal delivery surrounding them, they can turn innocent sentiments into aggressive, blaming, intimidating, or condescending messages.

- Need
- Must
- Now
- Have to
- Want
- You
- Your
- Tell (you)
- Talk to (you)
- Discuss
- Should
- Always
- Never
- Stop
- Calm down
- Relax
- Breathe
- I know how you feel

Many of the common phrases that we hear in the workplace include charged words—and are a common reason for miscommunications and misinterpretations. When paired with a certain vocal delivery or body language, these phrases can quickly create communication barriers. If you wound the listener with your words, you may create a wall that is difficult to break down.

The key is to try and avoid using finger-pointing words unless it's a strategic choice that you're making.

COACHING CORNER

Take a moment and consider—are there words or phrases that you say regularly that could be misinterpreted?

If so, choose two that you commit to trying to eliminate in the next seven days.

Just as the nonverbal gesture of finger-pointing can be perceived as aggressive or put someone on the defensive—while gesturing with an open hand can visually and subtly create a sense of welcoming and inclusivity—"open-handed" or "diplomatic words" can be substituted for their more finger-pointing counterparts.

Diplomatic Words

Using words that innately sound more diplomatic and tactful can instantly help to soften your message without shifting the meaning or making it sound weak.

- Pause

- Exchange

- Process

- Honor

- Acknowledge

- Recognize

- Share

- Highlight

- Explore

Take a look at the commonly used phrases listed in the left-hand column of the chart. Compare them to their more diplomatic, tactful alternatives on the right.

Commonly Used Phrases	Diplomatic, Tactful Alternatives
"You're wrong." "You don't know." "You don't understand." "You're not helping."	• "I see it through a different lens." • "Let's take another look." • "Share with me how you came to that conclusion." • "I see the issue a little differently." • "Can you highlight for me why you feel that way?" • "Let's look at the situation from a different angle." • "Why don't we focus on the desired outcome and see how we can get there." • "Let me clarify to make sure we are on the same page." • "Let's try something else . . ." • "Why don't we try it this way . . ." • "Walk me through the details."

Commonly Used Phrases	Diplomatic, Tactful Alternatives
"I disagree." "I would argue that . . ."	There are certain words where the word itself can set the tone and build the angst. The words "argue" and "disagree," in and of themselves, create the perception that there will be conflict or dissension. Avoid using words that innately reflect or increase tension. • "I hear you. I have <u>another perspective</u>." • "I <u>acknowledge</u> there are different options. Let me <u>share</u> mine with you." • "I see it from another perspective." • "Let me <u>highlight</u> for you how I see it." When responding to higher-ups, turn the statement into a question to show deference: • "Can I <u>share</u> with you how I see it? • "I'd like to <u>highlight</u> another option; is that fine?" • "If we <u>explore</u> some other options, we might find that ___ is true."
"Do you understand?" "Does that make sense?" "Are you following me?"	These questions are often interpreted as condescending. Better to eliminate them and replace them with: • "Does that sound doable?" • "How do you see next steps?" • "What is the next step as you see it?" • "What clarifications can I give?" • "I've given you a lot of information; what questions can I answer?" • "What part of the plan can I give more detail to?" • "What are your thoughts around what I've said?"

Commonly Used Phrases	Diplomatic, Tactful Alternatives
"So, we agree." "Are you in agreement?"	These phrases can often be interpreted as coerced or forced agreement—better to eliminate the sentence unless the context requires it.
"As I said before . . ." "As I already mentioned . . ." "Like I said . . ." "Like I told you earlier . . ." "As per my email from . . ." "As I stated in my email . . ."	These statements can be perceived as condescending and reprimanding—better to eliminate the sentences. Depending on your preference, you could simply repeat what you said or preface your message with: • "I'd like to emphasize the importance of . . ." • "Have you had a chance to see my email from . . ."
"Because I said so." "If I did not make myself clear . . ."	These phrases can be seen as belligerent and demeaning—better to eliminate the sentence.
"With all due respect, that's important but . . ."	• "That's an important point. We're headed in a different direction. I'm happy to explore this later."
"You need to calm down." "Everybody relax." "Geez, just breathe."	• "I'd like to acknowledge the level of frustration in the room." • "Let's take a five-minute break." • "There seems to be a lot of passionate conversation. Let's regroup and come back together." • "Let's agree to revisit this topic after we've had time to process the information." • "Let's take a moment to pause."

Commonly Used Phrases	Diplomatic, Tactful Alternatives
"That's not how we do things." "Can I be honest with you? That's not how it works around here."	• "I want to <u>acknowledge</u> your idea." • "Let me <u>share</u> something that has worked for *me*." • "That's a good technique. Let's apply that in a different situation." • "That's a good suggestion. Let's pursue that when the context is . . ." • "How about we try this." • "Let's remember that for next time." • "____ usually works well." • "Achieving _____ is often well received around here." • "I appreciate your ideas. Let's talk through this together."
"Let's just move on." "I'm gonna stop you." "Let's stay on track."	• "I see what you're saying. Let's come back to this." • "Thank you for sharing your idea. Can we agree to <u>exchange ideas</u> on this after we get through the agenda?" • "Let's circle back to this." • "I want to <u>acknowledge</u> your concern. In order to <u>honor</u> your time, let's schedule a different time to <u>explore</u> this." • "In order to hear your thoughts, let's make it a priority for the next agenda."

Commonly Used Phrases	Diplomatic, Tactful Alternatives
"You should get this done now." "I need you to do this by close of business."	• "I have an important item that I'd like you to handle." • "I _recognize_ that you have a lot on your plate. I'd like for you to make this a priority." • "I see you're very busy. You're the one who can get this done in the short amount of time that we have." • "Let's have ___ completed by close of business today. Any questions or concerns, I'm here." • "The deadline is close of business. Our goal is to meet it. Please handle ___."
"ASAP" "Let's table that." "Let's put that in the parking lot."	There are some phrases that have become so overly used, known as "word inflation," that they feel dismissive—better to eliminate the sentence.

Sometimes you're negatively labeled even when you had good intentions. This can be the result of mix messaging. Gesturing with a pointed finger while smiling, or avoiding eye contact while verbalizing your high level of confidence, can leave the recipient confused and wondering which message to believe.

Take it one step further. Even if you're saying something with positive verbal intentions, your message could still be misperceived as negative if the other person interprets your words differently.

Examples of verbal mix messaging include the following:

• "I _refuse_ to cut corners or dilute the quality of this project."
  The word "refuse" could be misperceived as stubborn and uncompromising, while the speaker's intention is to communicate his or her high degree of integrity and work ethic.

- *"I have a deep sense of <u>conviction</u> about this idea."*
  The word "conviction" could be misperceived as inflexible, closed-minded, or demanding; while the speaker's intention is to communicate loyalty, commitment, a deep belief, and unwavering confidence.

- *"I'm happy to <u>defend</u> the merits of this solution as a way to address the issue."*
  The word "defend" could be misperceived as belligerent, a "fight" mentality. It implies the speaker will not back down, while in fact the speaker's intention is to communicate his or her ability to articulate the facts, value, and evidence around the solution.

It's important to look at the choices you make from different perspectives. If there's any doubt about how you might come across to others, ask yourself, *"How could this be misperceived?"* This approach will help you to be more aware of how what you say or do could be viewed.

I know what you're thinking—you can't please everyone, nor would I want you to (it's an impossible task; trust me I've tried!). I don't want you to second-guess everything that you do; I want to support your success by giving you different ways to look at what you do—and the communication habits you've adapted over time.

There are many effective ways, as highlighted throughout the pages of this book, to soften your message, without sounding weak, losing your authority, or undermining yourself. You may also decide to continue using some of these words or phrases because they set a certain tone or communicate your message in a specific way. The most important take-away is that you're being a conscious communicator by making deliberate decisions as they relate to your communication.

The key is to be self-aware of what you're saying and how you're communicating it so that you eliminate undermining habits, communicate confidence, and speak with intention.

YOUR QUESTIONS ANSWERED

Some of the most common questions I'm asked when it comes to speaking with intention include:

1. *"How long does it take to eliminate filler words?"*

   If verbal habits can come, they can also go. Two strategies will help you to eliminate filler words: awareness and practice. You can see an improvement in using less filler words in as little as an hour (the length of a coaching session). To eliminate them completely will depend on your commitment to the techniques shared in this chapter.

   Here's your growth plan:

   - Increase self-awareness to which and when (which filler words you use and when you're most likely to use them).

   - Decide to self-monitor the habit (be committed that when you hear yourself using speech clutter, you actively pause or replay the sentence in your brain without the filler words—to ingrain the desired change in your memory).

   - Find opportunities to replace undermining words with more beneficial options. (Sitting back and responding is different from seeking out and initiating. The more you seek out opportunities to speak and practice, the greater the result will be.)

2. *"Is it okay to apologize if you meant to get an email to someone sooner? Or if you are responding to their email or phone call late?"*

   Unless your lack of response caused a problem for which you're now responsible, there's no need to say sorry. A solo sorry, without a real explanation, sounds meaningless:

   "Sorry, just saw your email."

   "Sorry, didn't know that you called."

There may also be a good reason why you didn't get to someone's email sooner. Regardless, no one wants to hear excuses. People want to be acknowledged and know that they matter. Try these responses instead:

"Thank you for your email. I wanted to get back to you sooner."

"So glad I found out that you called. I had no idea. Going forward, I've asked my assistant to capture messages in both an email and on a sticky note."

"Your emails are always on my priority list. Since I'm only getting to it now, it gives you a sense of how nonstop we've been over here."

You may notice that the examples I gave take more effort and time than simply saying "sorry." They're also much more meaningful.

3. *"If you don't want me to use the word "sorry," how can I show respect and courtesy if I mistakenly bump into someone?"*

Instead of saying "Oh, sorry," you can still show the same amount of care and respect by saying:

- "Excuse me."

- "Pardon me."

- "Are you okay?"

4. *"How do you stop someone from chitchatting on the side while you're presenting?"*

This question is a universal concern. Let's acknowledge that people who chitchat on the side while you're presenting—especially when it doesn't relate to the topic at hand or help to support you, are detracting from you, and are disruptive and disrespectful. Please don't ever be "that person." In an effort to curb this behavior, try these top tips:

- Involve this person in your presentation:

"Grace, I know you've been working on something similar. When I finish this section, I'd really appreciate you weighing in."

"I'll be covering ____today. Will you share your thoughts, Grace, on ____ when I get to it?"

- Make your presentation interactive:

  "As soon as I'm done sharing the information, I'd like to open it up for discussion on what parts of this plan you feel you can apply at work."

- Be engaging: body, voice, visuals.

- Set the "time tone" beforehand:

  "I want to acknowledge that we only have 30 minutes. To honor your time, I'll ask that we keep focused on the person speaking so we can move through the agenda."

  "Today I have five minutes of critical info to share. Can we silence phones and pause from laptops."

  "This next piece is something I'd like everyone to focus on."

Everything we say and do communicates a message. From the first impression that you make to the actions that you take, from your nonverbal and vocal communication to your ability to communicate the value that you bring—communicating your competence is key.

CHAPTER FIVE

COMMUNICATING YOUR COMPETENCE

Better to remain silent and be thought a fool
than to speak and to remove all doubt.
—ABRAHAM LINCOLN
Sixteenth president of the United States

When competence is the norm in your workplace, how do you distinguish yourself? On the surface, competence is the ability to do your job. It's the foundation for the initial value that you represent. If your goal is to distinguish yourself and make your mark at work, then it's essential to build on this foundation by demonstrating your ability in other core levels of competence.

Core Levels of Competence

Level 4: The ability to speak someone else's "language"

Level 3: The ability to navigate difficult conversations with diplomacy and tact

Level 2: The ability to handle common and awkward workplace situations

Level 1: The ability to self-promote and not self-sabotage

Foundation: The ability to do your job

Let's take a closer look at each of these levels.

FOUNDATION: THE ABILITY TO DO YOUR JOB

It's important that you have the know-how, capabilities, skills, and expertise to successfully carry out the responsibilities for which you were hired. You may not be perfectly prepared to address every aspect of the role— or even like some of what you have been tasked with; that may all come with commitment, learning, and time. If you accepted the role, you agree to uphold the responsibilities of the position and be fully committed to it.

It's important to know your strengths—and how they add value to your role and work environment. It's also important to be open to improving any limitations—so that they can become areas of opportunity and help to progress rather than diminish your success.

The key to laying a solid foundation
of competence is to be self-aware of the core
competencies you bring to that position.

As you assess these core competencies, you may decide you want to strengthen the foundational level of competence. If so, consider taking the following actions:

- **Attend professional development programs.** Making time for a lunch and learn, or an off-site class, is a great way to build rapport with colleagues, grow your professional network, and increase your knowledge and skills.

- **Take an assessment.** There are many communication, career, and personality assessments, including the SELF Profile, Myers-Briggs

Type Indicator, DiSC Assessment, and INSIGHT Inventory. Assessments can help you to better understand your strengths and highlight areas of growth and professional development.

- **Find a qualified mentor.** Not just anyone can be, or would want to be, a mentor. It's a commitment of time, and this individual needs to feel as if he or she can add value.

  A few years ago, I accepted an invitation to teach a communication class at a college in New York. Students sometimes ask me to write them letters of recommendation. If I can't do a student justice and add value (whether that's because I don't know the student well enough or the student doesn't reflect the characteristics or academic standards that I deem important), I have to graciously decline.

  The same guidelines hold true when looking for a mentor. Be specific about who you ask to be your mentor and know why you're asking this individual—even then this person may decline due to personal reasons or time restraints. That's okay because the fit must be right on both sides.

Some other important aspects of finding the right mentor include:

- Someone inside or external to your industry

- A person who will honor your confidence

- Someone who can offer unbiased guidance

- An individual who will advise on challenges and questions

- A person who has qualities you respect and admire

- A person who reflects a high level of expertise and skill

- Someone who can help you to develop personally and professionally

- An individual who can be a consistent point of contact so that there's continuity of support

It's incredibly helpful to have someone you can go to for guidance, ask questions of, and bounce ideas around with. Finding the *right* person is invaluable. It's important that you feel a connection with this person in order to build rapport and get the most out of the exchange. (Take a look back at Chapter 2 for a deeper dive into the mentor/mentee relationship.)

- **Surround yourself with CHAMPS.** CHAMPS are people who motivate you to reach a higher bar and who, through their own competencies, indirectly or directly highlight what more you could be doing to get to where you want to be. CHAMPS can be defined as individuals possessing all of the following core characteristics. They are:

  C = Connectors. The C's are individuals who are comfortable, and even enthused about, bringing people together through introductions, collaborations, and conversations. They are energized by interactions and see building rapport as an opportunity, not a chore.

  H = Honest. The H's pride themselves on transparency, truth, integrity, ethics, and having tough conversations— all with diplomacy and tact. They are authentic, have a high work ethic, and do what's right versus what's easy.

  A = Accomplished. A's have made a name for themselves and solidified their brand by consistently achieving. They have a track record of success. It doesn't mean they're always results-driven, goal-focused at all costs, or even successful at achieving every goal they set. It simply means they understand and are committed to the process of achieving the objective.

  M = Motivated. You may be, or work with, an M. M's are highly self-motivated, aspire to deliver quality work product, initiate, participate, and problem-solve, and they're not easily daunted by difficult scenarios or challenges that arise.

P = Professional. You can immediately recognize P's. They're the quintessential professional—visually, verbally, in their personal conduct, and most importantly because of how they interact with others. They take great pride in how they represent themselves, the company, and those associated with them—always with polish and courtesy.

S = Smart. The S's are individuals who are highly intelligent, are confident in their abilities, and think outside of the box. They enjoy solving a challenge, can look at an issue or question from different angles, and have such a strong grasp of their subject matter that it's immediately evident when they communicate.

COACHING CORNER

Who are the CHAMPS you surround yourself with?

Most CHAMPS are innately confident because of the attributes they possess. They also reflect one other essential characteristic—they're gracious.

The Art of Humility

Everyone you will ever meet knows something you don't.
—WILLIAM SANFORD NYE,
AKA BILL NYE THE SCIENCE GUY
An American science communicator
and mechanical engineer

There's a subtle secret that no one tells you on your quest for success: humility matters, and it can, ultimately, make a difference in your reputation, relationships, standing, and staying power. Think about some of the most successful people in our global sphere. When they're described, there are always two sentiments you hear about—their great successes and the reputations that surround them. How you wear success is very important.

There are distinct differences between two highly successful individuals. Those who wear success well are highly confident in their abilities. They also understand that their success wasn't achieved alone; as a result, they share the success, show appreciation, and always have an acute awareness that it can be taken away as quickly as it was achieved. These individuals graciously wear success.

Ability + Graciousness = Confidence

Those who do *not* wear success well are also highly confident in their abilities. The difference is that these individuals concurrently communicate, whether subtly or overtly, a disingenuousness or dismissiveness. They may have a superiority complex or be consumed with furthering their own advancement and success. They pretend to relate—without any real desire to. These individuals are beyond competitive—while wearing the facade of being laid back. They may appear distracted because they are "too busy" to focus on items other than their own, and they show a false sense of humility while constantly articulating the difference between themselves and others. These professionals arrogantly wear success.

Ability – Graciousness = Arrogance

Eventually, arrogance becomes a turnoff and starts to damage rapport, hurt reputation, and reduce opportunity—often overshadowing ability. The other extreme can also be detrimental—too much humility. Living in this realm, you could be misperceived as self-deprecating, weak, or irritating.

The key is to find the balance between
being successful and being gracious.

Once you have laid a strong foundation of competence, part of communicating your value is increasing others' awareness to it, which brings us to Level 1.

LEVEL 1: THE ABILITY TO SELF-PROMOTE AND NOT SELF-SABOTAGE

Visibility is a critical component of your success. As you assess Level 1 and your visibility within the organization or industry, if you want to strengthen this level, consider ways of putting yourself on someone's radar.

Communicating your value can take many forms and be achieved through different levels of intensity. Being aware of these options may help you to feel more comfortable with the idea of talking about yourself. To gain more visibility and reflect the value that you bring, try:

- **Grabbing coffee.** Invite someone out to coffee and exchange details about your roles and responsibilities. Learn about what you both do. A beverage or food can break down barriers because it offers another focus and can lessen the formality or pressure of a one-on-one situation.

- **Introducing yourself.** Find an opportunity to introduce yourself with a Credibility Statement (see Chapter 2 for more on Credibility Statements) instead of simply stating your name and title. This will help others to learn more about you.

- **Asking or agreeing to be part of a project.** Look for a high-profile or prestigious project that requires your skill set. Ask or agree to be part of it so that you add value while increasing your visibility.

- **Accepting an invitation.** Attend a professional development session recommended or supported by your leadership. By bringing back key points and sharing them with your team or department, you will have achieved three layers of visibility.

- **Volunteering your expertise.** Give your time, knowledge, and experience to an organization or school. By authentically helping others, you benefit. People outside of your industry and organization start to learn what you do.

- **Creating a knowledge-share.** Offer to coteach a lunch and learn or lend your expertise to a "stretch" project outside of your standard workload. This exchange allows you to share your knowledge and learn in the process.

As you consider activities that focus on increasing your visibility, remember to be selective and authentic. You don't want to overextend and then be perceived as resentful, insincere, or a pushover. Be seen doing things that you believe in—and not just for the sake of visibility.

The other essential aspect of Level 1 that will progress your success is to avoid self-sabotaging your value.

The Invisible Backpack

Did you know that you're wearing an "invisible backpack" right now? (I am too.) Every person that you come into contact with is wearing one. It contains every hurt, accomplishment, external influence, insult, life experience, award, compliment, and relationship you've ever encountered. We start to fill our backpacks from when we are very young, and without realizing it during our life's journey, we continuously add to them.

It's this invisible backpack that helps you to speak in front of a large group with poise and passion, try new adventures, take risks without the fear of failure, strive for achievement, respect the rights of others, tackle difficult conversations, and be emotionally resilient. It's also this same backpack that causes you to undermine yourself, react versus respond, criticize yourself, unconsciously self-sabotage, be judgmental of others, and doubt your abilities.

The experiences and influences that you carry around in this backpack have unconsciously become the main lens through which you see yourself, the world, and everyone and everything in it. When these thoughts and feelings are positive, they propel you to strive and thrive;

when the thoughts are negative, they become the mental and emotional clutter that weigh you down and, ultimately, act as barriers to your success.

COACHING CORNER

What are you carrying around right now that could be causing you to self-sabotage or undermine your value?

To address your invisible backpack and the thoughts and feelings within, take a look at the following techniques:

- **Be aware.** Realize that internal thoughts and feelings influence your current actions.

- **Recognize the dichotomy.** Increase awareness of the dual power of your thoughts and feelings. Some are positive and promote healing, while others are negative and fester within you. They guide how you see yourself as well as your responses, choices, interactions, and conversations.

- **Be kind to yourself.** Important change can take time.

- **Analyze and ask.** As you think about your experiences, people, or interactions, ask yourself:

  - *"What thought or feeling may be undermining me?"*

  - *"When did it start?"*

  - *"How has it been sabotaging me?"*

  - *"Why will it not serve me well going forward if I allow it to exist?"*

- **Decide.** Make a decision and commitment to no longer allow life-long negative judgments, thoughts, and feelings to dictate future outcomes.

During the course of conversations with our coaching clients, I quickly identify the thoughts and feelings that are acting as barriers to their success. Each individual starts to recognize how specific feelings may be undermining to him or her. They are then invited to "take off" the invisible backpacks containing these negative influences, put them in the conference room closet, and shut the door. This powerful image of taking off the invisible backpack is, in essence, removing the internal judgments that have caused him or her to self-sabotage. This starts to initiate a change in mindset and behavior.

Research reflects that visualization can be a very powerful tool in helping you to achieve your goals. In fact, people who picture their goals are 1.2 to 1.4 times more likely to achieve them.[1]

For many, also stuffed in their invisible backpacks is a fear known as "the imposter syndrome."

The Imposter Syndrome

Most people, at some point in their careers, have experienced self-doubt and thought, *"Can I do this?"* Self-doubt is a temporary feeling brought on by a specific event, task, project, or person. The imposter syndrome is different.

The imposter syndrome is a much deeper, often unspoken fear that lives within someone. It's the belief that you don't belong, nor do you have the right to be, where you are. It's the often unfounded fear that you're a fraud and that someone may discover that you don't deserve the job because you're not qualified. Many individuals suffering from the imposter syndrome *are* highly qualified. Therefore, it's critical to be aware of when your invisible backpack is misguiding your thoughts.

In order to address the imposter syndrome, focus on clearing the emotional clutter, countering these negative thoughts, and engaging in positive self-talk.

Self-Talk

Self-talk is your powerful inner voice—also known as your "inner monologue." It can either be positive, neutralizing negative thoughts, or negative, suffocating positive thinking.

Some professionals recommend just ignoring negative thoughts with the expectation that they'll eventually go away. I see it differently. When you try to ignore something, it often comes back stronger, distracting you even more and being relentless with its hold on you until you succumb. My guidance is to acknowledge the negative thought and then *immediately* counter it with your positive self-talk. When using positive self-talk, it's essential to cite specific examples of successes, qualifications, and positive feedback in order to counter and neutralize the negative thinking.

Neutralizing Negative Thoughts with Positive Self-Talk

- **Negative thought:** *I don't deserve this promotion.*

    Positive self-talk: Yes, I do. I have 15 years of experience in the marketing field, 6 years as a supervisor overseeing a staff of 3, and my performance evaluation last year was stellar.

- **Negative thought:** *I hate public speaking and am going to be awful.*

    Positive self-talk: I've given many presentations and have gotten positive feedback from the leaders in the room. I'm very good at holding their attention. I've got this.

- **Negative thought:** *I can't do this. There are so many more people here better qualified than I am. What am I doing?*

    Positive self-talk: I can do this. I have a degree in digital media, 10 years of industry-related experience, and they wouldn't have asked me to spearhead this project if they didn't think I was capable. They want me to be here leading this team.

COACHING CORNER

What could be a thought acting as a barrier to you?

How could you change the way you talk to yourself?

Once you have neutralized the negative impact and influence of your thoughts, you want to think in more positive terms. This will help you to clear the mental and emotional clutter for the long term by replacing it with a more positive mindset. It's critical to your continued success to be able to shift your mindset.

Shifting Your Mindset

If you live too long in a negative mental space, you become defined by it—and eventually perceived and labeled by others that way. By shifting your mindset, you're retraining the brain to get out of a negative thought pattern and think more positively. If you modify your thinking—and specifically the *initial* thought, the feelings around that thought will shift. Ultimately, this will lead to a different action or outcome. In order to achieve this, there's an important distinction to make: that it's not the event, interaction, or conversation that creates the mindset; it's *what we tell ourselves about it* that matters.

There's always a thought before the feeling. It's this initial thought that dictates how you feel and, ultimately, view and handle the event.

Thoughts lead to feelings.

Feelings create actions.

- **Initial thought:** *I am totally overwhelmed in this new position. There's so much for me to learn.*

    Related feelings: Worried, scared, annoyed, hopeless, frustrated, self-doubting

Potential actions: Speaking abruptly to others, isolating, communicating grave concern of inadequacy to your boss, never pursuing another promotion, walking around in a rushed or chaotic state, feeling dejected, or second-guessing decisions

- **Initial thought:** *Why does he always interrupt me when I'm speaking?*

  Related feelings: Annoyance, anger, frustration, retaliation, aggravation, exasperation

  Potential actions: Shut down, stop talking, glare angrily, sit silently with arms crossed, talk over him, interrupt him when he's speaking, complain about him, vent about the situation to others, lash out, tell him off, or talk to him

It's not always easy to get out of a negative thought pattern. You have a choice: you can be complacent in those thoughts and feelings, which negatively impact your behaviors—and perpetuate an unhealthy cycle. Or you can make a conscious decision to be in a much more productive, healthier mental space. To live in the latter, you must first modify your thinking, which will shift the feelings around your mentality; this will create another behavior pattern more than likely, resulting in a different outcome.

Let's shift the mindset . . .

- **Initial thought:** *I am totally overwhelmed in this new position. There's so much for me to learn.*

  Shifting your mindset: *Yes, there's a lot to learn, and I'm capable. Smart, talented, experienced leaders promoted me, and I have to trust they did so because they know I can do the job and handle the pressure. What do I need in order to prove them right?*

  Related feelings: Hope, worry, relief, focus, determination, permission

> **Potential actions:** Getting down to work, looking for a mentor, asking for feedback from leaders, delegating to team members, and sharing the concern with a friend

- **Initial thought:** *Why does he always interrupt me when I'm speaking?*

> **Shifting your mindset:** *He always interrupts everyone. He's really passionate about his job. Maybe he got interrupted or talked over when he was a kid, so that's all he knows—or there's a chance he doesn't even realize he's doing it. It's rude. I have a right to finish what I'm saying.*
>
> **Related feelings:** Resolve, annoyance, empathy, willingness, tolerance, conviction
>
> **Potential actions:** Finishing thought, communicating that he will have the floor in a few minutes, setting meeting tone and guidelines before the next brainstorming session, chatting with him to increase his awareness around his actions, allowing him to interrupt and then finding a way to interject back into the conversation, and building on his thoughts

COACHING CORNER

What is a recent interaction or conversation that you found upsetting?

Before you allow your next move to be dictated from that feeling, ask yourself:

- *How else could this individual's words or actions be interpreted?*

- *Could it have nothing to do with me and everything to do with him or her?*

> • *Is my invisible backpack influencing how I am interpreting this person's words or actions?*
>
> How have these questions shifted the way you're now looking at that recent interaction or conversation?

If you would like help to shift *your* mindset, take a look at the following techniques:

- **Practice adjusting your thoughts:**

    Initial thought: *If I make a mistake, I'll be so embarrassed.*

    Adjusted thought: If I make a mistake, I'll fix it.

    Initial thought: *I feel like I'm screaming.*

    Adjusted thought: I'm not screaming; I'm shy. I'm projecting my voice to be heard because what I'm saying is important.

- **Play devil's advocate.** In order to change the negative thinking, you want to challenge the thoughts:

    Negative thought: *If I forget what I want to say, I'll lose credibility.*

    Devil's advocate: Or . . . I'll keep going because the audience doesn't know what I plan on saying.

    Negative thought: *If I'm silent, people will think I'm stupid.*

    Devil's advocate: Or . . . People appreciate that I don't speak unless I have something to say. Or . . . People respect that I don't jump to an answer and instead wait until I have an accurate answer.

- **Gauge the validity of your current mindset.** An important aspect of being able to change negative thinking is understanding if the negative thought is still valid. This ensures that you're not living in an old mindset. If it's not valid and you're still operating from that old mindset, you could be self-sabotaging yourself.

> **Mindset:** I used to have an accent and people couldn't understand me.

> **Validity:** That was then, this is now.

> **Action:** I need to stop holding on to this fear, which is no longer valid.

- **Consider the worst-case scenario.** Sometimes we get so consumed by a negative thought that it becomes paralyzing. By asking ourselves, *What's the worst that will happen?* we can defuse the desperation, create a more rational response around the occurrence, and keep the direness of the event in perspective.

- **Try the "perspective wall."** Sometimes we are in too deep, up too close, or in a mindset for so long that we start to lose perspective. Step back and look at the occurrence from a distance. If you were giving someone else advice about it, what would you say? What course of action or solutions would you suggest? Does shifting roles or looking at the situation from another angle change your perspective?

- **Do it afraid.** By trying these strategies, you're embarking on a different way of thinking, of being. It can be scary, completely overwhelming, and uncomfortable. It can also create limitless possibilities of growth for you in ways you could never have imagined. Therefore, do it. Get outside of your comfort zone and—be afraid if you have to—simply start.

The key is that you're opting for a more positive path—by not allowing negative thoughts to dictate your responses.

> ### QUICK TIP
>
> ### Fake It Until You Become It
>
> The famous phrase *"Fake it until you make it"* never resonated with me. It seemed deceptive and inauthentic. Then famed Harvard University researcher and social psychologist Amy Cuddy coined the phrase *"Fake it until you become it."* Yes! Go through the motions— and if you truly believe in something that's not a natural tendency for you or within your comfort zone, stick with it, practice doing it until it becomes easier, more manageable—and it will. You may even find that you thrive at it. ·
>
> Shifting your mindset doesn't mean that you'll always be able to completely eliminate all doubt or negative thoughts and feelings.

It takes continued commitment to break the habit of negative thoughts—and ultimately retrain the brain to have a more positive mindset. The ability to modify your thinking is essential as you consider how best to navigate common and awkward workplace situations and establish your competence at Level 2.

LEVEL 2: THE ABILITY TO HANDLE COMMON AND AWKWARD WORKPLACE SITUATIONS

I've had the pleasure of meeting incredible people throughout my professional career. Out of these interactions, practical, impactful, and time-tested techniques have developed. I've taught these techniques in coaching sessions, group trainings, shared them during keynote talks, and applied them to my own conversations and interactions. I've honed them, over the years, to what they are now in this book.

My goal is to give you a different way of looking at these age-old issues and support your success in navigating these sticky workplace situations with more ease.

Saying No

"No" can be such a difficult word for some that rather than saying it, they take on the extra workload and run themselves into the ground. Others are very comfortable saying no because it's honest, concise, and efficient.

COACHING CORNER

Are you comfortable saying no?

How do you say no in a way that doesn't damage relationships?

Knowing a person's communication style, and delivering the message with diplomacy and tact, can make all the difference in maintaining rapport and avoiding giving offense when saying no.

Direct Communicators

Many direct communicators don't mind hearing the word "no" up front because it's in line with their concise, honest style of communication. Because these individuals aren't bothered hearing "no," they often think others feel the same. This is not always the case, and, instead, recipients may find the direct communicator's delivery abrupt. This could result in shifting the dynamic without the direct communicator knowing that offense was taken. Therefore, if you're a direct communicator, try offering an explanation to soften the severity.

"No, this isn't one of the options I can pursue because . . ."

"I understand what you're asking. No, we're unable to meet that request. Here's why . . ."

Indirect Communicators

Some individuals, who have a more indirect communication style, may not be comfortable using or hearing the word "no." If you have to respond "no" to an indirect individual, try finding other ways of saying no or making it the last word when you respond. When it's the first word said, it can often feel like rejection or sound too harsh and abrupt.

"Unfortunately, according to the policy that can't happen. This is because . . ."

"According to the policy, that can't happen, no. This is because . . ."

Saying No to a Boss or Leadership

(Um . . . let's agree this is a tough one.) The mentality of many leaders is that they've worked hard, been loyal, accomplished a great deal, and have earned and deserve their place at the helm. The expectation is that with this position should come respect, compliance, and deference.

If your boss asks you to handle a task and you're already beyond capacity, there are options for saying no—depending on your communication style and relationship with him or her. For example, to honor the hierarchy, one way to structure the message of a "no" is as a question.

Indirect response: *"Would you be willing to go through my current tasks and replace one of them with this new one?"*

Direct response: *"Could you go through my current list of projects and see which one we can reassign so I can take this on?"*

Direct response: *"It would help if you could reprioritize what I'm currently working on so I can dedicate the time you need to this agenda item. Okay?"*

Positioning "no" statements as questions to leadership achieves three objectives: showing deference; not actually needing to say the word "no," which could be uncomfortable and intimidating for some; and putting the action in their hands—which gives you some time. Asking leaders to take the time to figure out which tasks you can forgo may be too time-consuming for some, and they may give the task to someone else.

If you don't want to say no and are mindful that you can't say yes, suggest another option—such as co-handling the task with another person. Also, consider the person who's asking and the situation involved and ask yourself, *Is it worth saying no?*

If you really can't do a task, be able to articulate why—for example, your current workload, or you have a different expertise than what's needed to complete the request. If it's not in your expertise, it may be more time intensive than the asker realizes.

Saying No to Colleagues

Saying no to colleagues may or may not be easier than saying no to your boss or leader—especially if you're friendly with your colleagues. Being able to say no without actually using the word can be much more comfortable and less intimidating for some. In addition, honoring the importance of the request helps to soften your inability to assist.

> *"I hear that this is important to you. I really don't have the time with my current workload."*

> *"I really would like to take this on for you; I can't."*

> *"I'd want to dedicate sufficient time and focus to this in order to make sure it was done to my standards; there's no way I can do that right now with the number of tasks I have on my plate."*

Saying No to Direct Reports

It's not easy to bring an idea to a leader or make a request, because the fear is that it might not be well received. Any time you have to say no to your direct reports, or someone in a more junior position than you, be mindful. It may have been very intimidating for them to approach you with an idea in the first place, and it may be very discouraging to hear that idea get turned down. When saying no, keep in mind:

- **Seek balance.** As a leader, if you say no to everything, what are you saving yes for? Any time you can say yes, it helps to give more balance, maintain motivation, and offset the feelings in others that may arise when you have to say no.

- **Avoid a "Dead-End 'No.'"** A dead-end "no'" is when the decision-maker has given the asker a "no" without any other option or explanation. This response can be very demotivating and leave the questioner feeling dismissed.

- **Emphasize and explore.** Focus on articulating what you *can* do or have done and explore any alternative solutions that may get the asker closer to yes.

  "No, I wasn't able to get you the full raise. I still got you a raise."

  "We can't go that direction. What we can do is . . ."

  "I'm not authorized to . . . what I am authorized to do is . . ."

- **Tailor your message.** As a leader, you want to have consistent messaging and standards. How you deliver the message can be tailored to the "language"—communication style, of your direct reports. It's important to know that the delivery of "no" may be different depending on to whom you're responding.

Regardless of communication styles and positions, saying no with diplomacy and tact is incredibly important to effectively navigating this common, and often awkward, interaction. You may want to channel your inner Warren Buffett, who is rumored to say no to everything so that he can stay focused on the task at hand.

Saying No with Diplomacy and Tact

Take a look at the following techniques for reflecting diplomacy and tact when responding "no":

- Ask yourself, *does my delivery sound abrupt or harsh?* "No" is already a hard response for many to hear—the listener may be more sensitive to *how* it's being said.

- Are you explaining the "no"?

- Are you validating the question or request even though the answer may be no?

- Can your facial expressions be perceived as negative?

- Are you considering someone's feelings and need for respect when telling them no?

- Avoid giving excuses, long explanations, and apologizing.

- Try softening the "no" with a lighthearted response: *"My New Year's resolution was I'm only going to say three yeses. They've already been taken, so I can't."* (Be sincere, not sarcastic.)

- Were you ever at the receiving end of someone saying no? Think about what made it better for you and integrate that detail into your response.

Something else to consider is if you say yes when you really want to say no, you may end up resenting the person or task. If those feelings of resentment are visibly noticeable, they could end up shifting the dynamic.

This little word "no" holds a lot of power. It can make people feel uncomfortable if they have to say it or dismissed and rejected when they hear it. How you approach, position, and deliver the word "no," and to whom, is important in maintaining rapport.

Another situation that requires similar consideration is when you're sitting in a meeting or on a conference call and hear your boss or colleague state incorrect information. You have to be very careful how you handle the awkward situation of correcting incorrect information.

Correcting Incorrect Information

You don't want to embarrass the person who shared the incorrect information, and you still want to make sure the right information is heard or shared. It's a delicate balance, and the timing and choice of your actions depend on the position and rapport you have with the offender.

Colleagues and Direct Reports

It's often easier to correct incorrect information coming from a colleague, and even more so from a direct report, than it is a leader. Diplomacy and tact are always important elements of delivery—if you want to maintain rapport—especially if you're responding in front of others.

Boss / Leadership

(Again . . . not so easy!) If you highlight in front of others that your boss or a leader is incorrect, you may offend or be seen as overstepping your bounds. I recommend waiting until after the meeting to grab your boss's ear and share your thoughts.

If you have a very comfortable and trusting relationship with your boss, then another option is to graciously address the situation in the moment. The thought behind this choice is that if you know the information is wrong, others may as well. Your act of sharing the more accurate information in the moment may reinforce your loyalty to making sure your boss is always well-viewed. This is a decision you'll have to make based on your history and interactions with your boss, coupled with his or her personality.

If you're not sure how to navigate this situation or which option your boss would prefer, ask. When it comes to uncomfortable or awkward situations involving anyone—especially your boss or leadership, it's important to ask rather than assume. During your next one-on-one meeting with him or her or after a meeting when you're both walking out, check in:

> *"I always want to make sure that I'm representing you well. Part of achieving that for me is making sure I have your back when it comes to the accuracy of information. If I hear you say something that may not be exactly right, how would you like me to handle it?"*

Or

> *"I always want to have your back. If I hear you say something that may not be exactly right, how can I most respect you? Would you like me to interject in the moment, share my thoughts after the meeting, or . . . ?"*

Whether a boss, colleague, or direct report, if you decide to correct the incorrect information in the moment, try using one of the following phrases:

- *"Before we continue, I'd like to reemphasize that . . ."*

- *"There were a lot of facts given today; let me emphasize . . ."*

- *"The core information that really needs to be remembered is . . ."*
- *"It's very important to highlight . . ."*
- *"It's vital that we're all on the same page about . . ."*

Sometimes it's not incorrect information that you need to respond to; it's inappropriate comments or questions.

Responding to Inappropriate Comments or Questions

Humor is a strategy that can often break tension and defuse awkward situations. Over the years, I've learned, heard, and shared some great responses to inappropriate or awkward questions:

- *"How old are you?"*

    Response: *"Somewhere between 0 and death."* (with a smile)

- *"Who wants to take notes for us?"*

    Response: Silence.

    Unless your role is to take notes, volunteering for this action may diminish your role. If you volunteer, you may subconsciously be looked at differently, get pressured into taking notes consistently, or miss out on being part of the discussion because your relevance has shifted.

- *"Lydia, will you take notes for us?"*

    Response: *"Thank you for asking. I'd like to be able to focus on what's being said, and note-taking won't allow me to do that."*

Of course, if your boss asks you to take notes, then you need to make a decision that's best for the situation and rapport.

- *"You're younger than I thought . . ."*

    Response: *"Thank you. It's always nice to hear that I'm immune to aging."*

Response: *"Thank you. I appreciate hearing that I'm timeless."*

Response: *"It's nice to know I found the fountain of youth."*

- *"Wow, your hands are cold."*

    Response: *"Cold hands, warm heart."* (Thanks, Gram!)

- *"I never realized how short/small you are."*

    Response: *"Petite frame, big brain."*

Sometimes the tables get turned, and instead of responding to the awkwardness—*you* have created it.

I recently saw a work colleague at a social function. I hadn't seen her for almost a year. *"Congratulations!"* I said, as I smiled and eyed her baby bump. *"For what?"* she responded. I quickly assessed the situation and decided to keep my foot in my mouth to avoid making any further faux pas. I smiled and made mention of her kids.

You Put Your Foot in Your Mouth

Yes, it's awkward.

No, it's usually not intentional.

Yes, it's still awkward.

A couple of techniques to remember the next time you put your foot in your mouth:

- **Restate or explain.** If there's any way to recover in the moment—do. Giving clarification, rephrasing, or explaining what you meant will seem much more sincere and authentic if it happens right away rather than never or randomly later on.

- **Minimize your misstep.** Try to minimize your misstep by bridging to a related topic.

- **Apologize.** If what you said really was offensive, even if unintentional, apologize.

- **Use lighthearted humor to defuse.** Instead of making a joke about the blooper, which could make matters even worse, use lighthearted humor to ease the tension of what was just said, such as:

  "That's what no sleep will get you. You don't make mistakes often, so the next time you do, you get a pass from me."

- **Be kind to yourself.** We're human and mistakes happen—don't beat yourself up.

- **Be courageous.** Refrain from avoiding this person, no matter how strong the urge, because of *your* discomfort or embarrassment. Avoidance will only heighten the awkwardness and make the situation worse, as this person may start to wonder if the mistake was intentional or if you really don't like him or her.

Depending on the situation and the person involved, it can be very difficult to take back an awkward moment. What you *are* capable of taking back is hijacked conversation.

Taking Back Hijacked Conversation

Two of the questions I'm asked the most, and a huge point of contention for many, is *"What do you do when you're interrupted?"* and *"What happens when someone takes over the conversation?"*

As highlighted in Chapter 2, when we covered in detail the difference between interjecting and interrupting, you want to take back the conversation. If you don't stop people from interrupting you or hijacking the conversation, you're setting the tone that it's okay to do so. If you consistently allow people to do this, ask yourself, *Why am I allowing myself to be interrupted?* As you look to increase self-awareness, have people form an accurate perception of you, and communicate your competence, it's important that you know the reason behind your lack of action.

Here are some additional ways to diplomatically handle this uncomfortable situation:

- **Communicate confidence.** Smile, gesture with an open hand, and use a vocal delivery that's tactful and diplomatic.

- **Address the action.** Communicate to the interrupter that you still have a few more insights to share—rather than state that you're "not done speaking," which could be perceived as displaying attitude. If said in a courteous, tactful way, you have a chance to address this action, prevent others from echoing it, and avoid damaging rapport with the interrupter.

  > *"Grace, I want to hear what you have to say. As soon as I'm done sharing my thoughts, I'll turn it over to you (open hand toward interrupter)."*

  If you say that you'll turn the conversation over to someone, please do. Your follow-through will immediately reflect that you stick to your word. "Walking the talk" always helps to strengthen your credibility in the eyes of others. It may also help to prevent this person from interrupting again; when people know they'll be given an opportunity to speak, they're less apt to interrupt in order to be heard.

- **Bridge back to you.** If you're interrupted and the person hijacks the conversation, your goal is to find a way to "bridge" back to your point so that you can take back the floor.

  Similar to the Brooklyn Bridge, London Bridge, or Golden Gate Bridge, which get you from one point to another (unless you're caught in New York City rush-hour traffic), there are statements that do the same. Use the following statements to interject yourself back into the conversation and redirect the conversation to wherever it was before the interruption:

  - *"Before we move on, I'd like to add . . ."*

  - *"This conversation supports my previous point that . . ."*

  - *"If we could go back a few minutes to . . ."*

- *"Here's the underlying issue that we need to focus on . . ."*

- *"_____ is important; it's also important for us to circle-back to . . ."*

- *"I'd like to revisit my initial suggestion about . . ."*

- **Solidify your reputation.** By communicating confidently, addressing the interruption, and integrating important elements, such as using the person's name and acknowledging that the interrupter has something to contribute, you send three powerful messages to the group:

  - Message #1 exudes your self-confidence. It shows that you value what you're saying and would like to finish your thought.

  - Message #2 conveys that you "see" this person. By acknowledging that he or she has something to say, you show humility, generosity, and self-assurance.

  - Message #3 reflects your professionalism. You can navigate awkward or uncomfortable interactions with courtesy, graciousness, and skill.

If the Interrupter Is Your Boss

If the interrupter is your boss, evaluate the situation and your response to it:

- Do you have a good rapport with your boss and feel comfortable asking him or her if you can continue?

- Can you set the expectation before the meeting? If so, before you meet, ask your boss if you can share your thoughts and then turn it over to him or her, which may help to deter interruptions.

- You may want to let the interruption happen if you feel saying something may cause dissension, embarrassment, or difficulties for you later.

It's important to address uncomfortable or awkward situations so that you don't appear indifferent. Your lack of action could mistakenly translate into your indifference to them. The same initiative you showed with taking back hijacked conversations, you also want to show when it comes to addressing misdirected questions.

Questions Are Being Directed to Your Boss—Not You

There are many reasons why someone may be directing questions to your boss, questions that you're capable of answering and have the role and responsibility to field. Some of those reasons may have nothing to do with you and everything to do with their quest for visibility.

If you find yourself in this situation, it's an important conversation to have with your boss. It can be an opportunity to reaffirm your competence and why you're capable of answering these questions. It can also help to strengthen the rapport between you and your leader because, instead of letting this annoyance fester, you're asking your leader to clarify expectations and support your success.

When broaching this conversation, tailor your delivery to the rapport you have with your boss and his or her communication style, and be mindful not to sound confrontational. Try some of the following conversation starters:

- *"In this morning's meeting, I noticed that John was directing his questions to you. As the project manager on the account, going forward could I answer the questions?"*

- *Is it fine if I field them first and then turn it over to you so that you can add your thoughts? My concern is that if I don't answer, the other consultants will start to get confused about who to bring their questions to."*

- *"I've started to notice, in the last few meetings, that people are now talking over me when I speak and wanting to hear your answer. Would you be willing, at the next meeting, to set the tone that any questions regarding this project are directed to me and that my direction will reflect your views?"*

- *"If I'm silent, my concern is that people will think I don't know. Do you mind if I answer the questions?"*

When it comes to answering questions, sometimes you don't have the answer. That's okay. You don't need to have all the answers to communicate competence—you simply need to know who is a resource or where to find the information.

You're Asked a Question—You Don't Know the Answer

If you're asked a question and don't have the answer, the following strategies will still allow you to communicate your competence in a large group atmosphere, team meeting, or during a casual conversation:

- **Stay calm and confident.** It can be extremely nerve-racking to be asked a question, especially by leadership or in front of others, and not feel confident that you're able to answer. Keep calm in both your body and voice. The audience has no idea you're uncomfortable unless you "tell" them.

- **Share what you *do* know.** Communicate an aspect of the answer or emphasize what you do know around the issue or topic. This could satisfy the asker and also highlights your skillful handling of an uncomfortable situation.

  "Based on what we know so far, my idea around this is . . ."

  "With the research that was done, here are my thoughts . . ."

- **Offer action and time.** When you truly have no idea what to say, committing to a concrete action within a specific amount of time reflects your respect for the asker, work ethic, and competence. Try the following statements:

  "I want to give you an accurate answer. Let me do a deep dive and get back to you later today."

"To answer this question requires additional research. I'll get back to you before noon tomorrow."

"The information we have regarding your question needs to be confirmed. There are a few key people that I'll connect with on this. Would it be fine to get back to you by the end of the week?"

Use the word *accurate*, when at all possible. It's very hard for someone to argue with you, or pester you for an answer, when you want to give them accuracy. In addition, if you're going to use the technique of action and time, it's essential that you follow through on both—or instead of communicating your competence, you'll have others questioning it.

- **Avoid fatal faux pas.** There are certain tendencies you should steer clear of when you're asked a question you don't know.

  - Giving an answer that is an exaggeration, lie, or unfounded assumption

  - Repeatedly responding, *"I don't know, I'll have to get back to you."*

  - Stating a dead-end "I don't know." Similarly to a dead-end no, a dead-end "I don't know" gives the asker no other option or explanation. This response can immediately create uncertainty around your credibility.

    Alternatively, you can let the questioner know you will connect with someone, conduct the specific fact-finding needed, or put together your thoughts and send them to him or her: *"I'll get together with Alice, who is the expert in that area, and I'll get back to you this afternoon."*

    Be specific as to the action you're taking and the time it will take you. After not being able to answer the question, you don't want the asker feeling any uncertainty around your getting back to him or her and when that will happen.

Sometimes it's less about the conversation or situation that creates discomfort and more about the person.

Dealing with "Difficult" People

I traveled to Canada recently to give a keynote speech at a client's annual conference. As we all filed onto the chartered van, on walked Chris (yep, his real name). Chris was an American in his late thirties who had obviously been drinking. He made it clear from the moment the chartered van doors closed that he was going to make this ride fun—for him. It started off with his extra-loud voice offering alcohol in the back of the bus. It continued with his insistence that we all smile for a "group photo." After an hour and a half of what became vulgarities, harassing a fellow passenger, and a one-man show of random noises and outbursts, Chris was kicked off the van.

I never have to see Chris again. You may work with someone similar—which makes matters much worse since you have to interact with this person on a regular basis.

It's not easy to rise above when you're faced with someone who's rude, disrespectful, belligerent, immature, or a bully—who may lie, take credit, or say one thing and do another; who projects onto you his or her own issues and then makes you feel like you're the crazy one; or who refuses to contribute because it's "outside of the job description." I call these individuals "toxic" and "energy suckers" because having to be around and interact with them is demotivating, draining, and harmful to our emotional and mental health.

It's important to acknowledge that it's *extremely* difficult—and almost impossible—not to allow these individuals to affect you in a negative way. In an effort to protect yourself and be prepared when you come into contact with these individuals, take a look at the following strategies:

- **Increase awareness and tolerance.** Increase awareness that some "difficult" individuals may not see themselves that way. They may only be "difficult" because they see things differently than others do, don't feel included, or have a core need that's not being met.

Increased understanding, tolerance, empathy, and speaking their "language" may go a long way with these individuals in breaking down barriers and shifting behaviors.

- **Maintain composure.** Avoid putting *your* perception in jeopardy, even in this difficult situation, by being *civil.*

   Being *civil*—concise and polite—is different than *courteous,* which reflects a warmth and thoughtful politeness—and is necessary for building rapport. Since your goal is not to engage more than absolutely necessary with these individuals, being civil is appropriate.

- **Limit interactions.** Try to interact with difficult people as little as possible. If you let these people impact you, you have fueled their power—and you're left drained and changed.

- **Keep a record.** Start to record, with dates, locations, and people present, any negative interactions with, responses from, or offenses by this person. If the situation escalates, you'll want to bring it to the attention of your leader or HR. They'll want to know specific circumstances surrounding your complaint—and your greatest advantage will be that because you kept a detailed record, you can speak in facts.

Someone Intentionally Being Disrespectful

It can be a tormenting situation if you have to work with someone who's intentionally or subtly being disrespectful. As hard as it is, try to remember that people like this eventually sabotage themselves, get a negative reputation, and become alienated because no one wants the drama of working with them.

To relieve some of the stress caused by this person, you can try:

- **Steering clear.** If your job does *not* require you to interact with this person, there's no need to engage.

- **Focusing on the task.** If your job *does* require you to interact with this person, then focus on the task—there's no need for small talk or to spend extra time with him or her.

- **Putting a layer between you and this person.** If you're in a position to indirectly distance yourself by assigning someone else to have direct contact with this individual, do.

- **Removing *them* from the situation.** If this person is your direct report, or you have any influence around having this person reassigned, transferred, or removed—seriously consider it. If you're feeling the negativity from this person, so are others. Part of your role as a leader is to create a safe working environment for your team members.

- **Removing *yourself* from the situation.** If this person is abusive, disrespectful, or manipulative, and nothing has been done by management to curtail the behavior, remove yourself from the situation. Is it fair that you have to be the one to leave, change, or remove yourself? No. Nothing is more important than your mental, emotional, and physical health.

When this person is your boss, you have a difficult choice to make. You either preserve your sanity and protect yourself by changing reporting lines, departments, or companies—or you stay. Complaining about this person may or may not yield the results you're looking for—especially since he or she has been allowed to get away with this behavior up until this point. Going to Human Resources gets it on record; it's also important to be prepared for potential retaliation. While this could make your life more difficult, you'll have the backing of a team of professionals who specialize in matters like this. Either way, you know better than anyone what the right choice is for you.

The Office Bully

It's very clear in work environments across the globe that adult bullies exist. The only solution is a leader who doesn't tolerate the behavior, holds the bully accountable, and sets a precedent that the behavior will not be tolerated—and that without question it will be addressed. Sadly, this is not often how bullying is handled.

The problem is that in many workplaces, the office bully not only exists—he or she thrives. According to a National Survey from The

Workplace Bullying and Trauma Institute (WBTI), 60 million Americans are affected by workplace bullying.[2]

A bully is allowed to exist for a myriad of reasons. He's the boss, and no one above is doing anything about it; she's the rainmaker and it's all about the bottom line; he's the only one who knows how to do what he does; she's sued her previous employer and the current company is navigating from a place of fear; or she has a close rapport with a leader, which is enough to keep her "safe."

Regardless of the reason, the person being bullied often dreads going to work, is consumed by discomfort, suffers mental and emotional anguish, can't sleep, and can often feel alienated, depressed, and consumed by the behavior. The longer the behavior is allowed to exist and the bully remains unchallenged, the more serious the symptoms for the person being bullied become—with many victims often suffering from post-traumatic stress disorder.

In order to maintain your mental and emotional health and not allow this toxic situation to rub your nerves raw, take a look at the following techniques for dealing with bullies—in some small way they may help to ease the situation:

- **Show a strong and confident exterior.** Bullies bully, in part, because they can. The minute you sense this behavior, show a strong and confident exterior—even if you're cringing inside. Bullies get bored if they can't scare, intimidate, or rile their prey and will often stop.

- **Stand up for yourself.** Bullies bully, in part, because *they* have been bullied. It's their way of finding an outlet for their internal turmoil of hurt, anger, or humiliation. They want to do to others what has been done to them. Whatever their reason, you don't deserve to be their target. Set the tone, through your responses, that you refuse to tolerate this behavior.

- **Speak to your leader.** Let your leader know or, if your leader is complacent or the bully *is* your leader, tell Human Resources. Make the decision-makers aware of what's happening to you and potentially others. In addition, document what's been going on.

You may be asked for specifics or to show a paper trail—and you want to be prepared.

- **Summon your support system.** Another reason to put energy toward building an internal network and establishing your competence at work is that highly regarded people will often find themselves being listened to and supported by leadership. Ask your support system to back you by helping to deal with the situation and lending their influence to rectifying it.

- **Remove yourself from the situation.** Bullies try to intimidate others into siding with them. The more people, the more power they feel they can wield. Knowing that this person needs the coerced support of others to act this way makes him or her a real coward. Still, if the intimidation or group bullying continues, remove yourself from the situation—your mental, emotional, and physical safety is most important.

When this person is your boss, you have a difficult choice to make. If you stay, do all you can to improve the situation within the chain of command and by lodging a formal complaint with Human Resources.

*The key is to make sure that **you** are never the bully.*

Someone Consistently Unresponsive

If someone is consistently unresponsive, you have no control over why this person is not responding. What you can control is *how* you communicate with him or her.

- **Speak their "language."** A good rule of thumb, when dealing with an unresponsive person, is to pick the mode of communication that he or she prefers. If this individual works in IT and you know the whole department doesn't have time for in-person chats, send an email or pick up the phone. A quick way to find out what works best for someone is to ask.

- **Vary communication.** Try different modes of communication when dealing with an unresponsive person. When it comes to important matters or tight deadlines, this guideline helps to eliminate excuses that can easily accompany one-way communication: *"I didn't receive the email," "I wasn't at my desk when you came by,"* or *"I couldn't pick up the call."*

- **Acknowledge.** If you're comfortable having the conversation, acknowledge the difficulty you've been having in trying to reach this person and find out why he or she is being unresponsive. There's a chance it has nothing to do with you.

- **Try three times.** Try reaching out to this person three times if it's not a time-sensitive issue. If it *is* a time-sensitive request, then escalation may be the only option.

When dealing with difficult situations and people, you may feel completely at a loss—that nothing is within your control. Remember you *are* in control—the one thing in your control is how you choose to deal with it.

COACHING CORNER

Who are three people in your life, and specifically in your work world, who energize, refuel, and inspire you?

Part of communicating your competence is your ability not to shy away from uncomfortable situations, many of which involve difficult conversations.

LEVEL 3: THE ABILITY TO NAVIGATE DIFFICULT CONVERSATIONS WITH DIPLOMACY AND TACT

Whether dealing with someone who is difficult, or a colleague whom you really like, having those tough conversations is never easy, and that's why it's Level 3.

Having Difficult Conversations

A big source of discomfort for many is having a difficult conversation. They equate it with conflict—and most individuals shy away from conflict. Therefore, when a difficult conversation needs to take place, most people are left nervous, uncomfortable, or dreading the thought. The worry keeps them up at night, or they avoid having the conversation altogether—and the feelings or issues never get addressed or resolved. It's a hard place to be in—angst or avoidance.

Some experts are trying to shift the way we look at difficult conversations, from being something that worries us to something that empowers us, by referring to them as "fierce conversations" or "courageous conversations." I agree with this line of thinking—remember, a shift in mindset *can* yield different results.

The key is to have strategies for handling these moments, reflect gravitas, and practice the conversation beforehand.

Have Strategies

For many professionals, having strategies for approaching the conversation can be empowering. They know that doing it well can be the means by which they solve and resolve.

Take a look at strategies you may want to consider before your next difficult conversation:

- **Pre-conversation considerations.** In order to make the most of the meeting, there are important details to keep in mind:

  - **Deciding to have the conversation.** It's important that you reflect commitment and confidence around the process of having the conversation. This approach can add impact to what you're saying and help to set a tone of importance.

    › Knowing why you're having the conversation. The why— and the direct impact you hope to see—are two important elements in achieving a positive outcome. Why are you having the conversation? Is it to increase awareness, resolve an issue, clarify understanding, or inform?

> What is your desired outcome?

- Having the conversation in person. Once you decide to have the conversation, having it in person is always ideal. You have much more opportunity to reflect the message you intend, when your body language and voice can work together to convey your thoughts and feelings.

  > If there's no way to have this conversation in person or you're more effective on the phone, because you want to avoid publicly blushing or losing your nerve, then do what works best for you.

  > Either way, give your conversation partner some sense of the topic so that he or she doesn't feel blindsided—unless you have specific reasons for keeping it quiet (i.e., a firing).

  > If after careful consideration, you decide that no good will come from having the conversation or that it will not benefit you in the end, venting to a trusted friend or mentor may bring you the resolution you need.

- **Choosing the location.** Where you have the meeting sends a message. Aim for someplace in line with the tone you're trying to convey. Depending on the context of why you're having the conversation and the hierarchy involved, there are four main options:

  > *Your office:* If you ask the person to come into your office, it reflects a certain level of formality. It could also feel intimidating for him or her—which may or may not be your goal.

  > *His or her office:* Similar to a sports team, home-turf advantage is always more comfortable—it can also hold more natural distractions for this person. Popping into his or her

office can also communicate a more casual approach to the conversation.

> *Neutral space:* If you want your conversation partner to feel on equal footing, or you're trying to create a clean slate, you may opt to have it in a neutral space.

> *Informal tone:* Some difficult conversations are more effective when they're approached in a casual manner versus a more formalized structure. If this is the case, having the conversation while walking to pick up lunch or grab a coffee may be the way to go.

- **Timing the conversation.** Keep in mind that the conversation will be more impactful if you have it as close to the occurrence as possible.

> Try to have this conversation as soon as possible following the behavior, decision, or event.

> Choose a time that will allow the recipient to be most focused. Avoid scheduling a difficult conversation during lunchtime, Friday afternoon, Monday morning, or at the end of the day—unless you're firing someone. People look forward to lunch and need time to reenergize and refuel. By close of business, they are more than likely mentally exhausted and ready to leave work behind.

Reflect Gravitas

Staying calm, clear, and confident in moments of discomfort, and reflecting grace under pressure, can be extremely difficult. It can also defuse tension and prevent the conversation from emotionally escalating.

- **Techniques for reflecting gravitas:**

  - *Be mentally prepared.* Calmness comes from within. When you intentionally remove distractions and are mentally present, you can seem more composed.

- *Exude confident posture.* Nonverbal messaging can speak volumes. To reflect presence, focus on making eye contact and exhibiting body language that is still, open, and takes up space.

- *Use vocal delivery elements.* Reinforce and support your confident presence and composure through the voice. Speak in a lower, slower voice, which can reduce misinterpretations and infuse calmness. Use a voice that reflects the tone of the conversation and have solid breath behind your words so you don't sound nervous or weak.

- *Respond instead of reacting.* If something is said that you didn't expect to hear or don't agree with, intentionally pause before responding. Think about what you want to say. Give the information a chance to move away from your emotional center to the more logical place in your brain. Your words have impact and will linger in the air and in the mind of the listener—choose your words wisely.

- *Listen.* Listening is the hardest thing to do when you feel attacked or disagree with someone. Speaking over someone, or interrupting the speaker, will undermine your presence and gravitas because you'll appear riled. Listening authentically also sets the tone that you, too, would like this same level of respect when speaking. The context of the conversation will determine how much listening you do.

- *Be courteous.* Staying courteous, or at a minimum civil, depending on the context of the conversation, is within your control. If the other person's behavior is inappropriate or rude, you can feel confident knowing you maintained your demeanor—as you continued or quickly concluded.

Practice the Conversation Beforehand

There are four steps to think about when having a difficult conversation. Becoming familiar with them, and practicing them prior to the actual discussion, will help you to depersonalize the conversation. It will also help you to focus on the outcome, reflect confidence, and avoid feeling flustered or at a loss for words.

- **Step 1: Start the conversation.** You want to start the conversation within a few minutes of sitting down.

  - Avoid catching up and making small talk with the recipient. You can briefly thank this individual for meeting with you.

    A colleague of mine recently recounted a story about being called into his manager's office. The reason was not previously disclosed, so there was some uncertainty from his perspective. The manager asked about his daughter's dance recital that had taken place a few days before. The two men spoke for a while, swapping stories about their weekends. Then the manager said, *"We have to let you go."*

    In sharing this story with me, my colleague couldn't fathom why his manager would make small talk with him, instead of getting right to the bad news—especially because the initial chitchat left him believing nothing was wrong.

  - Start the meeting by getting right to the point of the conversation, within the first five minutes.

    Unless you've previously shared the purpose of the meeting, the recipient is probably already feeling uncomfortable or uncertain. Prolonging the focus of why you're there, will only draw out the dialogue and infuse more angst. The purpose of a difficult conversation is not to punish the recipient or make him or her feel undue anxiety.

- **Step 2: Share observations or concerns.** Sharing your observations or concerns is the reason why you're having this conversation. Focus on delivering your message in a clear, concise, factual manner.

  - Articulate your message without making your conversation partner feel judged.

The goal of the conversation is to resolve, inform, or clarify. If this individual feels judged or attacked, he or she may immediately become defensive and shut down before anything worthwhile happens.

Some phrases to start with include:

"This week I observed . . ."

"My concern is that I heard . . ."

"I'd like to share my thoughts about . . ."

"Yesterday I experienced you . . ."

"It's come to my attention . . ."

- Be mindful to use *"It's come to my attention . . ."* sparingly. Most people will immediately wonder who brought it to your attention—and why you believe that person. Used too often, this statement can undermine your credibility because it's hearsay and could be perceived as favoritism or you taking sides.

- **Step 3: Articulate impact or explain consequences.** Articulating the impact or potential consequences of this individual's behavior helps him or her to understand the seriousness and importance of the conversation.

Some phrases to continue with include:

"I'd like to share with you the impact of . . ."

"Here's how I see the impact of . . ."

"_____ has had severe consequences for us. Let me share with you a few of them."

"What's at stake if we _____ is . . ."

- Be concise when articulating the impact and consequences.

- Tailor the "impact statement" to the receiver in order for it to resonate most with him or her. Think about how you can position the statement so that the recipient cares about what you're saying.

- Explain the impact or consequences on the three main spheres in this person's work environment—him or her, the organization, and you. You want to share the impact on each— starting with what the person cares most about—himself or herself.

Example of a Difficult Conversation: Steps 1–3

One of our coaching clients shared his concern that he's not consistently invited to the monthly board meetings and feels he needs to be. We sat together to script what he could say in order to be heard. We did so in a way that was nonconfrontational for him and so that he was comfortable approaching this topic with his leadership—using the steps highlighted.

"Good morning, _____. Thanks for sitting down with me.

I'd like to share my thoughts around the monthly board meetings.

I'm concerned that I haven't been invited to attend these meetings on a consistent basis. There'd be value in my being there.

I know that this upcoming reconstruction project is incredibly important to you. If I'm not at the meetings, I can't provide insights on the reconstruction ideas, and I know you see this as your legacy with the club. If an unnecessary idea proceeds, it could waste members' money or force the club to be over budget. And if I'm not able to share my thoughts as the project manager, I'll be doing work I potentially don't believe in.

The consequence is if something turns out wrong, I'll be blamed because I went along with it."

- **Step 4: Incorporate empathy.** As highlighted, empathy is a powerful tool. It can prevent a difficult conversation from escalating, empower listeners, and differentiate leaders.

  It can also quickly gather important information from your conversation partner, make him or her feel heard, and shift what could easily become a one-sided lecture into a two-way conversation.

  After you've shared your concerns and articulated the potential impact, you can invite this individual to share his or her thoughts. By incorporating empathy, you're reflecting *"I want to understand..."*

  - Ask your conversation partner, *"Do you see it this way?"* By giving this person a chance to respond, you may learn something you didn't know—which could shift how you approach the rest of the conversation.

    There are three main responses you could receive:

    > *"Yes."* If the recipient agrees with what you have said, eureka! Now you can agree to next steps and move forward with shared understanding. If this difficult conversation took place because of a behavioral issue, create an Action Plan together; this way the employee knows that you support his or her success and that he or she will be held accountable for the change.

    > *"No."* If the recipient doesn't agree with you, there may be a legitimate reason of which you're not aware. People who receive a "no" often directly or unconsciously shut down the conversation. Avoid the urge to do so by continuing on the path of empathy and asking the recipient, *"How do you see it?"* Whether or not you agree with what's being said, let this person answer uninterrupted.

    > *Confrontational response or repeat offender.* Some difficult conversations can get heated—or even confrontational, depending on the context, personalities involved, and

severity of the situation. If that's the case, it's important to stop the conversation and either revisit it at a later time, or immediately state how the individual will be held accountable.

If this person is a repeat offender, having displayed the behavior or made the mistake before, skip the empathy. Instead, be direct about sharing how this person will be held accountable.

It's very important to your credibility to hold this person accountable in the ways you state to him or her. The person will know you're serious, as will those on the outside of the situation looking in.

There are a couple of other important points to consider when planning and practicing your conversation:

Being on the Receiving End

When *you're* on the receiving end of a difficult conversation:

- If empathy is not incorporated and you're not given the opportunity to share your thoughts, initiate an opening by saying, *"I hear you. I'd like to share with you how I see it."*

Conversing with Your Boss

When your difficult conversation is with *your boss or leader*:

- If you're concerned about delivering your "impact statement" because it may seem too forward or if you're not given the opportunity to weigh in, one approach is to initiate an opening while also showing respect by *asking* to share it, *"Can I share with you how I see it?"* or *"I'd like to share with you how I see it ..."* or *"Can I share with you the impact of ... ?"*

- If your conversation is difficult because you're asking your leader for something (such as a raise) and you find that you have shared understanding, make your ask. Be clear and concise with what you want.

- Another option is to make a statement while "asking" through facial expressions, vocal inflection, and words. This reflects your confidence and clarity about the ask and next steps while showing deference, not direction, to leadership.

> *"I'd like to be included in this month's board meeting."* (Use raised eyebrows to reflect a question.)

> *"I'd like to join tonight's meeting, if that's fine."* (Words of approval balance the statement.)

Avoid going through the whole conversation and then leaving the opportunity on the table—make your ask. (You don't want to run the entire New York City marathon and then stop right before you cross the finish line!)

COACHING CORNER

Who do you need to have a difficult conversation with?

How will you position it differently, knowing what you now know?

There's another aspect to having a difficult conversation that's important to mention—what if the conversation is emotional for you?

Emotional Conversations

If you experienced an upsetting situation or were hurt by someone, be aware of the degree to which emotions are affecting you. Are the emotions simmering at the surface? If so, it's in your best interest to wait. Table the conversation until your feelings are not as new or raw. Conversations colored by emotion may not be heard or even taken as seriously as ones that are more matter-of-fact.

If you've decided that an issue is important enough to bring up to your leadership, be strategic with how you position it.

Here are some guidelines to consider when broaching an emotionally charged topic:

- **Organize your message.** Have a general outline or plan of what you want to say. Depersonalizing the situation helps to reduce the emotion.

- **Practice out loud.** When you say and hear the words coming out of your mouth, the body gets used to saying the emotional piece. Repetition seems to lessen emotion.

- **Broach business before the emotional situation.** If you have other agenda items to cover, broach them first. Avoid addressing the emotional piece as the first topic you cover—unless it's the only topic you plan on speaking about. This approach reinforces your value, and it's also more likely to spark your manager's sincere interest when you shift the conversation to a more personal nature.

- **Avoid undermining yourself.** You made a decision that the topic was important enough to address; now commit to it so that the listener takes you seriously. Refrain from apologizing, downplaying, joking about, or feeling awkward around initiating the conversation.

Commitment + Confidence = Being Taken Seriously

LEVEL 4: THE ABILITY TO SPEAK SOMEONE ELSE'S "LANGUAGE"

Part of what prevents a difficult conversation from escalating, or an awkward situation from spiraling, is the ability to acknowledge the other person's point of view and speak in terms that resonate with him or her. Being able to speak someone else's "language," is a high-level skill that will highlight your competence, help to increase your influencing power, and build rapport. Welcome to Level 4.

Speaking Someone's "Language"

People will forget what you said, people will forget what you did,
but people will never forget how you made them feel.
—MAYA ANGELOU
American poet and civil rights activist

There are many different communication styles. Knowing that different people have different ways of communicating is incredibly important in making sure whatever you say is getting heard. Learning to speak someone's "language" means figuring out *what* this person's communication style is, *how* he or she likes to be communicated with, and what's *important* to him or her. It's a significant factor in being seen as a conscious communicator.

Communication assessments, as shared earlier in the chapter, are an effective, efficient way to increase self-awareness of your own communication style as well as those of your colleagues. As a leader, having your team take an assessment is also a great teambuilding exercise. Since most of us can't walk around the office randomly handing out communication assessments to colleagues in an attempt to gain insight, it's incredibly important to be able to read others.

Ability to Read Your Audience

In order to speak the communication "language" of others, it's essential that you're able to read and understand others' cues. Learning about people by observing, conversing, or listening will increase your awareness of what they value; it will also help you to better understand how best to communicate with someone. Let's example some of the most successful people in the world to reflect how words can be a clue into what someone values and, therefore, how best to communicate with him or her.

In God we trust. All others bring data.
—MICHAEL BLOOMBERG
former New York City mayor and American businessman

A call lasting longer than 30 seconds,
I find, has diminishing returns.
—ALAN "ACE" GREENBERG
former chairman of Bear Stearns and
author of *The Rise and Fall of Bear Stearns*

Be your best self.
—OPRAH WINFREY
American media mogul

In addition to listening, observing people's body language, tendencies, and interactions are other quick cues that can offer insight. There are some key questions to think about when trying to determine people's communication style:

- Are they detail-oriented?

- Do they have a deep technical knowledge or expertise?

- Are they fast-paced or more methodically-paced?

- Do they have a high need to direct and control?

- Are they happy being behind the scenes, or do they seek the spotlight?

- Are they comfortable leading, or do they prefer to be part of the team?

- Do they like to work in groups or prefer solo projects?

- Are they people-oriented or task-focused?

- Are they enthusiastic and energetic or efficient and low-key?

- Would they appreciate facts, planning, and research or get inspired by exploratory conversation and brainstorming?

- Is having quality relationships a priority for them, or are they results-driven and outcome-based?

- Do they speak and act quickly or move in a measured way?

- Are they direct?

- Are they feelings-based or facts-focused?

Once you know how someone likes to be communicated with or what's important to him or her, your value increases—because commonality builds rapport. In addition, you now know how to structure your message to best resonate with this individual. When your message resonates with someone, there's only upside.

When speaking about this topic, I'm consistently asked to address how someone can communicate in the "language" of others and still be authentic to who they are.

An Oath of Authenticity

Tailoring, or being able to "flex" your style to most effectively communicate with someone else, doesn't diminish you or require you to change who you are. In fact, it enhances your value because it underscores your ability to interact effectively with a variety of people. In addition, it reflects that you're a conscious communicator because you've deliberately decided to practice the mindset of self-awareness and professional growth. *That* will distinguish you.

The key is to authentically want to speak other people's "languages" and "flex" your style to most effectively communicate with them.

Flexing Your Style

When done successfully, flexing your style is a gesture that can result in infinite positives: it can increase tolerance, foster rapport, prevent miscommunications (and misperceptions), get you closer to yes, give you influencing power, more easily bridge differences, defuse tension, create commonalities, and sustain rapport.

To practice flexing your style, take a look at the following strategies:

- **Results-focused.** To work effectively with colleagues who are results-focused, set benchmarks and milestones, create a time-management checklist, put a process in place, work hard, position what you want to say in terms of results, and be organized.

- **Relationship-centered.** To communicate effectively with colleagues who are more relationship-centered, volunteer with them, join your company's extracurricular sports team, be part of a community club, send emails or cards for birthdays and special occasions, make more small talk instead of getting right down to business, remember important information someone shared with you, invite people to lunch or coffee, have a candy dish on your desk, offer to help, and be a mentor.

- **Uncertain.** If you're unsure how to flex to someone's style and best communicate with him or her, ask:

    "What is your ideal time of day to meet?"

    "How do you like to be communicated with? Email, phone, in person?"

    "What aspect of the research would you like me to address?"

When sharing the concept of flexing, there are two questions I most often receive:

"Why do I have to flex my style? Let them flex theirs."

"What are some ways to communicate effectively with higher-ups?"

Fair questions. Important distinctions.

Flexing to Others

If you wait for others to flex to your communication style, you could be waiting a long time. This is because many individuals don't know about the concept of flexing. In addition, why give the power of your success to someone else? If you know there's a technique that can make a positive difference for you, why wait for someone else to progress your success?

The success of your communication with senior leadership depends on many factors.

Speaking the "Language" of Leadership

A few key techniques that will help you speak the "language" of higher-ups effectively include:

- **Highlight the WIIFT (= What's In It For Them).** By immediately tailoring your message to the goals and strategic initiatives of your leadership, you create instant value. You quickly become more engaging so that they want to listen.

- **Be concise.** Higher-ups don't often have time or patience for long-windedness or to sift through a great deal of information to get to the part that interests them. Remember the universally used acronym BLOT = Bottom Line On Top and Franklin Delano Roosevelt's mantra *"Be sincere; be brief; be seated."*

- **Practice extemporaneous structure.** Make sure higher-ups feel confident that you have full knowledge, awareness, and control of what's in your realm. Being able to give updates, or speak about topics off the cuff, helps to reinforce their confidence in you.

- **Share the impact on the listener.** A high-level executive, at a world-renowned company, shared with me that immediately after our coaching session, she was going into a pivotal meeting. She needed to convince her two colleagues why her idea was the one they should pursue. After giving me the backstory and dynamic between the other leaders, it was clear to me that she didn't need to approach this meeting with an objective to "convince." Her colleagues weren't holding steadfast to their positions; they simply needed to hear why she believed so deeply in her idea. This meeting was about her positioning—what the impact would be if they didn't pursue her idea. Understanding the impact on higher-ups, and positioning your message that way, makes what you have to say more relevant and valuable.

"The impact of going in this direction is . . ."

"Here's my concern in doing . . ."

"Here's what could transpire if we . . ."

In addition, no leader wants to be blindsided. By speaking in terms of impact, you may add another layer of understanding—or highlight a different perspective than initially seen by the leader. This results in helping him or her to avoid pitfalls and feel confident that the right decision is being made.

- **Prioritize and position.** With time being the most precious commodity, the minute you waste it, the perception of you and what you have to say dramatically shifts. Focus on getting to the core of what you want to communicate quickly, by prioritizing and positioning it as: "911"-Solution-Outcome.

  - *"911."* Pare down what you want to say to the "911." Share the absolutely critical information that the leader needs to know.

  - *Solution.* Offer a solution or two. If the "911" you shared needs a solution, avoid only communicating the problem to the leader. Come to the conversation with some ideas so that you're perceived as a problem-solver and not a complainer.

  - *Outcome.* Understand the solutions—or conduct a feasibility study, if appropriate—so that you can give the anticipated outcome if your idea *is* pursued. Leaders want complete ideas and will likely adopt a new one only when they can see the merits of a solution and can visualize the result.

- **Offer three options and your imprint.** In general, leaders don't want to be inundated with the minutiae, hear the deep dive details, or read through the required research. Most leaders prefer to know that the due diligence was done and that what's being presented to them are the best options supported by facts. In order to raise the bar and increase your competence in the eyes of your leadership, be clear on which of the three options you'd support— and why.

- Do the research.

- Give three options.

- Share the option you recommend.

- Let your leader decide.

This process allows leaders to feel most confident making a decision because you've been thorough. You're proving that you have done the research, analyzed the options, given thought to the best one—and can articulate, with facts, why you feel your choice is ideal.

- **Ask.** If you're not sure how best to communicate with a leader, ask.

  "Where would you like me to start?

  "In order to make the most of our time, would you like me to begin with _____ or _____?"

  "Which of the three agenda items is most important to you?"

Thinking along these lines will allow you to reflect competence because you can quickly and concisely get to the heart of what matters most.

Knowing how best to communicate your competence will set you apart and help you to leave a positive, lasting impression on those with whom you interact.

YOUR QUESTIONS ANSWERED

Here are some of the frequently asked questions I've received regarding common and awkward situations:

1. *"How do you disagree diplomatically?"*

   If you want to disagree with someone while maintaining rapport and an open dialogue, it's essential that you disagree with diplomacy and tact.

This way the other person doesn't get offended or embarrassed and shut down, and you reduce the likelihood that the conversation will escalate and become argumentative.

In addition to the strategies shared in Chapter 4, here are some guidelines to consider:

- First, show acknowledgment. Before you share your thoughts about what was said, let the other person know that you heard them. When people feel acknowledged, they're often more open to what you have to say.

    "I can see _____ is very important to you."

    "I hear that your concern is . . ."

- Next, articulate what you want to say in a way that is valuable to the listener: WIIFT.

    "I can see _____ is very important to you; that's why I want to highlight that . . ."

    "I hear your concern is . . . so it's important that we take a look at it from the perspective of . . ."

- Lastly, share how you see things unfolding:

    "The impact of going with option A could be . . ."

    "Here's my concern in doing . . ."

    "What could transpire if we . . . is . . ."

**The key is that you can still be direct—if that's
your "language"—and diplomatic.**

2. *"My boss consistently schedules meetings with me and a few minutes into them starts typing an email. How would you handle this?"*

For both of you, time is valuable. I'd guide you to speak up, using a respectful sincere tone, such as:

"I want to acknowledge you're busy; is this still a good time for us to meet?"

"I know you're being pulled in many different directions. Would it help to revisit this later today?"

"I'm happy to excuse myself and come back in 10 minutes if you need this time."

3. **"How do you negotiate salary or ask for more money?"**

Your approach will depend on the context of the situation, how confident you are in pushing the envelope, and the personality of the person you're asking. It's most important to have as much information as possible before you have the conversation.

Try these strategies:

- **Do your research.** What do other individuals with your skill sets, experience, and education make?

- **Ask your mentor or trusted advisor.** *"What does a successful person in this position make?"*

- **Provide accomplishments.** When asking for more money *while employed* at the organization, come to the decision-maker with a bulleted list of five of your most impressive accomplishments. Be able to clearly speak to them and articulate the value that you bring.

  If you've proved your value and the benefit that you bring, ask for what you want.

- **Defer when asked.** When asked about your salary requirements *while applying or interviewing* for a job, the fear is that it will quickly be the deciding factor before you can communicate the value that you bring. Therefore, if asked early on, try to defer and find out more information by asking:

  "With the specific experience and skills that I bring to the table, can you tell me the salary you have in mind?"

*"Can you share the range of compensation for this
position?"*

- **Negotiate the total package.** Consider negotiating the total
compensation package instead of focusing solely on salary.
The salary may be lower than you'd like; in conjunction with
the rest of the compensation package, it may be a great offer.

    *"This is a great opportunity. I'd really like for this to be a
    win/win. I understand where you're coming from having
    a salary cap. If we can start there and then explore the
    other aspects of the compensation package, I'm open."*

- **Suggest an alternative.** If the salary is lower than you'd like,
try to find a fair compromise by suggesting an alternative
option:

    *"You've offered me the market rate. With my level of
    experience, I'd ask you to consider _____."*

    *"Thank you for your offer. You've offered me _____. I've
    worked hard to have my ability reflect _____. Would you
    be open to compromising at _____?"*

    *"You've seen what I'm capable of (either because he or
    she has read through your CV or seen you in action). My
    expectation would be in the ballpark of ____ , based on
    what I bring to the table."*

- **When pushed for an answer.** If pushed to answer about your
current salary, answer directly if you're comfortable stating it
and are confident with the way the conversation is going—the
last thing you want to do is evade a direct question to the annoyance of the asker.

    *"I'm very excited to take this job. What I bring is . . . What
    is expected of me is . . . For that, I'd like to make____."*

Another option is to let the decision-maker know, before you answer the question, that you don't want to make a lateral move.

> *"My goal is not to make a lateral move when it comes to my title or salary. I currently make _____.*

If you're afraid to lose the opportunity due to the salary conversation, you can also think about sharing a range from a little above your bare minimum to your ideal amount.

> *"I have a great deal more experience than I did when my salary was initially determined, which puts me in the range of _____ to _____.*

- **Stay positive.** Try not to be disappointed if you don't get the answer you wanted. No doesn't always mean no; it can also mean "not now" or reposition the ask in a different way so that the person can say yes or wants to think about it and revert back.

4. **"I'm uncomfortable when people come to me to gossip. What could I say?"**

Gossiping is one of the biggest ways to break trust and damage rapport. There's no need to engage in it—especially in the workplace, where the impact from a negative perception can have multiple, severe, and ongoing consequences.

When responding to someone who wants to gossip, try:

- Changing the subject

- Staying quiet and still—not participating visually or verbally

- Responding with statements such as:

> *"I'm not in a position to speak on that."* (My personal favorite)

> *"I enjoy connecting with you on so many things. I prefer to steer clear of intra-office drama."*

> *"I don't know the situation—and even if I did, I prefer not to be involved."*

> *"I really can't weigh in. I'm out of the loop on what's happening."*

- Using humor to defuse—and then changing the subject:

> *"I stream all of my drama through Netflix. Speaking of which, have you seen the show _____?"*

Articulating your value in ways that are tailored to what's important to others; navigating common and awkward workplace situations with confidence, calm, and professionalism; conducting yourself in an effective way during a difficult conversation; and recognizing the communication "language" of others so that they feel at ease around you and see the benefit that you bring will also help to establish your credibility.

CHAPTER **SIX**

ESTABLISHING CREDIBILITY

Watch your thoughts, for they become words.
Watch your words, for they become actions.
Watch your actions, for they become your habits.
Watch your habits, for they become your character.
And watch your character, for it becomes your destiny.
What we think, we become.

—FRANK OUTLAW
Late president of the Bi-Lo Stores[1]

You could probably name an individual who is knowledgeable, skilled, and excels at his or her job. This person would be considered by all accounts technically competent. This person may also be manipulative, have questionable intentions, and live in the gray area because it fosters quicker results. Do you *fully* trust this person?

Probably not, because this person lacks character.

You may also know someone who is guided by rules, has the best of intentions, and lives life with authenticity and transparency—by all accounts exhibiting a high level of character. This person may also be mediocre at his or her job, inconsistent with the quality of work he or she submits, and lack the abilities and knowledge required to achieve results. Do you *completely* trust this person?

More than likely no. This person lacks competence.

Credibility is the ability to inspire belief in your words, actions, capabilities, and decisions, which in turn results in your being seen as trustworthy. As a result of being trusted, you have the ability to build and sustain rapport, establish a high "likability factor," and enjoy more influencing power. Therefore, to truly be seen as credible, you must possess both a high degree of character *and* competence.

COACHING CORNER

Are you seen as credible in your organization right now?

Do you want to be seen as more credible going forward?

People's perceptions of you often become your reality and, ultimately, your reputation. Fair or unfair, it's other people who have the power to promote you, give you a raise, approve additional headcount for your department, find the money to support your professional growth and development, and determine your credibility.

Let's delve deeper into the concept of establishing credibility by taking a look at the two essential elements that define it—competence and character.

ESTABLISHING COMPETENCE

In Chapter 5, we highlighted the importance of communicating your competence. You may possess a great deal of expertise and business acumen, yet if no one knows your value, your competence could be in question. It's essential that you're visibly reflecting the core competencies that you want others to know you possess.

Your technical savvy and ability to do the job can be gauged fairly quickly. As can your ability to professionally handle yourself in a variety of business situations, present yourself with polish and professionalism, speak the listener's "language," and conduct yourself in a manner that makes others feel comfortable around you.

If you want to further strengthen this element of credibility, take a look at the following actions to help you consciously communicate your value:

- Set, verbalize, and achieve goals.

- Speak up.

- Invest in yourself to keep developing.

- Create a list of accomplishments.

- Get comfortable with successes.

- Practice saying things about yourself.

- Help colleagues to speak on your behalf.

- Keep your résumé current.

- Cultivate a network.

Distinguishing yourself and your abilities takes commitment and consistency—it can also be exhausting. Constantly striving, thriving, and advancing, or maintaining the same intensity, can deplete you physically and drain you mentally. This is the dilemma of work/life balance.

COACHING CORNER

Do you currently have a work/life balance?

If yes, how did you achieve it?

How do you maintain it?

If no, what in your life is misaligned?

If you could shift one or two things to create the balance, what would you change?

Work/Life Balance

"Does work/life balance exist?"

"Can you have it all?"

These questions come up in our sessions and are many times posed by successful women who have to sacrifice other areas of their lives to consistently achieve. They're on the treadmill of life, often spreading themselves too thin and pushing at a pace that seems unsustainable for the long term. Something has to give. For high-achieving individuals, when something has to be sacrificed to maintain this intensity, it's usually a matter of self-sacrifice or neglect of their personal life.

What fuels this misalignment? Is it a need to exceed expectations, conquer the challenge, or something in the "invisible backpack"? Is fear a factor? No matter the answer, if you're feeling it's time to rebalance work and life or you're getting burned out, try these strategies:

- **Shift your mindset through positive self-talk.** You're the CEO of your own life. *You* decide what your life looks like. Answer the following questions to gain insight into what could change:

  - If you could talk to your younger self, what would you say?
  - What do you want for your future self?
  - What allows you to pause and enjoy the moment?

- **Have an accountability partner.** Share your goals around work/life balance with someone in your network or inner circle. Ask this person to check in with you periodically on your progress toward achieving these goals.

- **Meet with a mentor.** Speaking to a neutral person can offer perspective and ease work-related pressures. It can also prevent you from bringing tense feelings home—which could add stress to other areas of your life.

- **Do something you love.** Make a list of things that you love to do or that make you feel relaxed, such as:

- Watch your favorite show or movie

- Hit the gym or do an extracurricular activity

- Laugh more

- Plan a vacation

- Meet up with friends

- Read a non-work-related book or magazine

- **Schedule stress-relievers in advance.** According to research from the *New York Times*, *planning* something can bring a similar satisfaction to you as doing the actual activity or event itself.[2] Here are a few ideas to get you started:

  - Schedule one day off each month.

  - Choose one night per week to go home early.

  - Decide that one weekend a month will be email- or technology-free.

  - Plan a vacation.

  - Arrange a time to meet with a therapist or someone who soothes you.

All things being equal, you may decide that where you are in your life, or with the career goals that you've set for yourself, a work/life balance is *not* possible right now (note to self). One specific aspect may need more of your focus and attention at this juncture—and that is okay.

**The key is that you're making the deliberate
decision to live your life as you do.**

A time may come when your priorities shift and you set your sights on something completely different. Ultimately, it's your choice. Don't apologize for the life that you live or the choices that you've made. Realize that you *can* have it all; it may not be at the same time.

Being able to communicate a high level of competence will quickly distinguish you. It's still only half of the equation. In order to establish credibility, you want to be visible consistently reflecting a strong character.

ESTABLISHING CHARACTER

While competence can be assessed fairly quickly, character seems to take longer to gauge. It takes time to assess someone's intentions, core values, reliability, and level of integrity. Character is also often revealed during times of crisis or quandary. Think about whether you:

Do what is right—versus what is easy

Step up—instead of stepping out or stepping over

Do what is appropriate—when no one is looking

Have good intentions—and are cognizant of when you don't

Are honest and authentic—consistently

Know what you stand for—and don't easily flip-flop to be more popular

Communicating your character is a core component of establishing credibility. Here are some key behaviors to strengthen and reflect your character:

- Offering empathy
- Being helpful
- Reflecting reliability
- Walking the talk

- Being authentic

- Speaking truth *with diplomacy and tact*

- Taking ownership of mistakes

- Being loyal

- Reflecting honesty

- Having good intentions

- Being kind

- Following up and following through

- Showing commitment

- Responding versus reacting

- Being consistent

The key to character is consistently exhibiting positive behaviors.

Demonstrating character helps to build trust, strengthen relationships, and enrich your network. Strong networks are invaluable in communicating your competence and character and, ultimately, establishing your credibility.

COACHING CORNER

How do you help others to feel comfortable around you?

What are your strategies for building and sustaining rapport?

Building and Sustaining Rapport

Rapport is like a plant. It will thrive if you nurture it. Consciously show-ing commitment to relationships and nurturing them is the core compo-nent to building *and* sustaining rapport.

It takes focus, time, energy, and commitment to invest in someone else. That's why it's essential that you build and sustain rapport and nur-ture relationships only with people you genuinely like. Some techniques for building or sustaining rapport include:

Being an Effective Listener

- Building rapport: Listening and sharing

- Sustaining rapport: Knowing how that person needs you to listen. It shows care, interest, and that you're invested in the relationship.

Emphasizing Commonalities

- Building rapport: Identifying commonalities, such as having the same vision, sharing the same goals, or possessing similar person-ality traits

- Sustaining rapport: finding opportunities to emphasize, experi-ence, or explore those similarities

Showing Interest

- Building rapport: Showing someone attention

- Sustaining rapport: Reflecting genuine interest in who people are and what they do or care about

Exchanging Knowledge

- Building rapport: Asking someone's opinion or sharing your thoughts

- Sustaining rapport: Exchanging knowledge by asking him or her to teach you something and offering to reciprocate

Turning a Tendency into a Tradition

- Building rapport: Meeting once or twice

- Sustaining rapport: Getting together regularly

Your ability to nurture relationships will eventually allow you to cultivate a network of reliable people who know you well and can be a source of information, consider you a resource, and speak on your behalf to others. This will give your credibility another level of visibility.

Cultivating a Network

Professionals with strong networks have staying power. A strong support system can give you insights, tools, and resources to succeed in a project or your day-to-day job responsibilities. These colleagues can attest to your abilities and contributions, speaking positively on your behalf. This word of mouth, these testimonials, can be a very powerful tool in progressing your success and solidifying your standing among decision makers and influencers.

COACHING CORNER

Have you cultivated a network?

What are two or three ways that you've established "staying power" with these individuals?

The key is to know whom to include in
your inner circle and network.

When Character and Competence
Are Disconnected

Knowing whom to include in your network will prevent you from undermining the credibility you're trying to establish. There are people who are highly competent with extremely questionable character. This poses a problem because the competence can mask the deficit in character. There are others who don't realize their extreme personalities make interactions difficult. A third group of individuals exhibit behaviors or reactions that can make you feel like you're the problem—when rationally you know you're not.

One of the fastest ways to damage rapport, break trust, and undermine your credibility is associating with someone who is irrational, erratic, malicious, or manipulative (those "toxic" individuals we talked about). Trust takes time to build, relationships require effort and commitment to nurture—and there are behaviors and actions that can destroy both instantly:

- Gossiping

- Showing favoritism

- Threatening or blaming

- Forming cliques

- Being manipulative

- Having a negative attitude

- Being condescending

- Lying or cheating

- Yelling

- Playing the victim

- Reacting instead of responding

- Embarrassing others

- Making false claims and accusations

- Consistently failing

Your credibility is based on affiliations—and even the *perception* of those affiliations. In general, which are you more apt to remember—the positive or the negative? For most, a compliment is heard, an insult is remembered; a win is celebrated momentarily, a mistake is regurgitated indefinitely. The same is true with relationships—more often than not the negative person overshadows the positive person.

How you navigate certain circumstances can enhance or undermine your credibility. Some of the less obvious situations that you want to be mindful of include the following:

Knowing What You Don't Know

Part of building trust is being realistic and transparent about what you don't know—without undermining yourself. If it would benefit you, it may be appropriate to seek someone's guidance or insight. Asking for this input can strengthen a relationship, since you're showing trust in that colleague. Some great questions to ask are:

"What am I not thinking of or did I leave out?"

"What else could we be doing to move the needle on this?"

*"What questions would **you** be asking?"*

Questioning Your Credibility

Whether you or someone else is questioning your credibility, avoid telling people what you don't have and letting self-doubt undermine you and direct your actions.

A leader in one of our sessions worked closely with the scientists in her lab. She was very experienced, knowledgeable, and respected. When introducing herself to other scientists, many of whom had PhDs, she would say,

"I'm not a scientist, but I look forward to working with you."

She allowed her cheat sheet of insecurities, about not having a PhD, to lessen the strength of what she did have—what she was bringing to the situation. Instead of highlighting what you perceive to be inadequacies or insufficiencies, shift the focus onto what you do know, emphasize what you can do, and share your commitment to learn.

"Nice to meet you. I also have 20 years in the industry. I look forward to working with you."

When you share with others what you *can* provide—on what they can rely, they feel more comfortable, clear, and certain; certainty builds trust.

Leading with Credibility

You will not lose credibility, even as a leader, because you don't know everything—especially if you're liked.

With a new position, department, team, manager, or set of responsibilities comes a learning curve. This is a given, and in most situations, taking some time to understand the expectations will not undermine your credibility. What will do you a disservice is that you're not doing everything possible to get up to speed or progress to the next level by meeting the demands of the new opportunity.

Your team needs to believe in you—that what you say, you do; if you solicit ideas, you consider them; if ideas are submitted and not accepted, you share why; any opportunity to put a team member's suggestion into play, you will; and that you recognize their efforts and hear what they need. By being supportive and transparent, you give others a legitimate, honest understanding of the situation, which in turn builds trust. These actions can even-out the balance as you get up to speed with the technical side.

**The key is that building trust comes
with being respected and liked.**

Overcompensating

Communicating your competence is very different from overselling the value that you bring.

In your quest to achieve work/life balance, you may decide to take time for yourself. One detail to be aware of is that if you're uncomfortable about taking this time, you may unconsciously feel the need to overcompensate—to overexplain, convince others of your worth, and prove your value. This subconscious need to convince people of your competence can have the exact opposite effect from the one you intend.

This response can also end up creating doubt around what you can deliver. People trust you when they feel and see that you trust yourself. If you're overselling, it could communicate that you're trying to convince yourself, which in turn makes others question you and your ability—and all of a sudden you have created doubt where doubt didn't exist.

This feeling of discomfort can also manifest as needing to hold yourself to a higher standard than others, or setting unrealistic expectations to prove your capability, which can also set you up indirectly for failure.

Exhibiting Etiquette

Maintaining all of your best practices, especially when the virtual boundaries of email and social media are easier to blend, will allow you to reflect a high level of competence and character— especially when you're faced with multiple communication points *at once*.

You may be one of the countless professionals who are under constant and intense time constraints, work on highly visible projects with high risk and reward, manage tens of thousands, or even millions, of dollars in budget, and get inundated with an overwhelming number of emails while you attend nonstop meetings. The pressure on you is great.

In addition, since every second counts, you may find yourself with someone sitting at your desk while you see work-related emails or Slack messages—a team messaging app—coming in, your desk phone rings, and you're hearing your work cell ping, signifying new texts that may require your immediate attention.

What, or whom, do you attend to first? It's a difficult balance that can quickly put you in an uncomfortable position. You have a few options that are considered proper etiquette:

- First, you can opt to treat the person in front of you as the most important interaction happening—and continue focusing on him or her.

- Second, you can let the person in front of you know that "this is important" (referring to your interaction with him or her) and mention you only need a moment to pick up the call to see if it's an urgent matter. Honor that: if the call is not urgent, let the person on the other end know you have someone sitting with you and offer a specific time when you'll call him or her back.

- Third, if appropriate, or if you find that you're too distracted to continue speaking with the person, you can start to wrap up the conversation or ask him or her if you can resume at a different time.

Some tips for maintaining the credibility you've established when communicating over email include:

- Use the person's name.

- Put a few key words in the subject line (avoid starting your message there).

- Write in the recipient's "language."

- Include a personalized closing—other than relying on your signature block—such as *"Looking forward to hearing your thoughts."*

- Use punctuation—limit exclamation marks.

Prioritize Your Email

If you're overwhelmed by the sheer number of emails you receive, prioritize your emails by organizing them into folders so that you can easily recognize and respond to them. Flagging everything as important doesn't quickly help you to discern where to start—nor does it reduce the feeling of being overwhelmed when you look at them. Folders could be categorized as: VVIP, Important, and Respond to Later. This will help you to quickly know whom to respond to first. These categories can be defined as:

- **VVIP = a Very, Very Important Person, Project, Predicament.** This term encompasses more than just emails from highly influential or inaccessible clients or leaders. It also means all emails that require your *immediate* attention and response.

- **Important.** If you tag an email "Important," it requires your attention or response relatively soon—it's not considered critical.

- **Respond to Later.** If you place emails into this category, the email is on your radar for response at a time when you have addressed all other issues. Place emails in this folder if they don't require a time-sensitive response—and be mindful to respond as promptly as realistically possible.

If you find that you're CC'd on numerous email chains that don't pertain to you, ask the senders to remove you going forward, or consider coming up with one phrase that you email to *all* of the senders at once (make sure to put their addresses in the BCC line if they're external to the company to honor their privacy). An example response is: "Thanks for your email. Since I don't have an active role in this particular project, I'm going to hold back on responding to the email chain. Please reach out directly if there's something you need."

Establishing credibility requires a multidimensional approach. If there's something you want to change because it could be undermining you, make a mental note and either practice doing it or continue eliminating it until it becomes a natural part of who you are. As twentieth-century English writer Virginia Woolf once wrote, *"A self that goes on changing is a self that goes on living."* Having a mindset of self-awareness, self-motivation, and proactively moving toward a place of growth will allow you to make the change authentically.

The key is to consciously choose to replace the thing that could be undermining you.

YOUR QUESTIONS ANSWERED

Questions I am often asked about establishing credibility include:

1. *"How can I get my ideas heard and be more influential?"*

   First and foremost, cultivate strong, trusting relationships. When people trust you, they're typically more open to your opinions and ideas. You can also try the following strategies:

   - Know your audience.

   - Focus on the WIIFT and the value to, and impact on, them.

   - Address their concerns.

   - Emphasize what's at stake and areas that may be impacted if your idea is not pursued.

   - Position your idea in the listener's "language."

- Communicate your competence so that they take your ideas seriously.

- Use compelling language supported by facts, data, and potential outcomes.

- Ensure a substantive vocal delivery.

- Make others feel something—avoid relying solely on numbers and facts.

2. *"Any advice for an introvert when it comes to building rapport?"*

Meeting people you don't know or putting time into nurturing a relationship takes energy. It can be exhausting for everyone, especially if you consider yourself more of an introvert.

To truly connect with someone and build rapport, give yourself a realistic goal. Start with a measurable target, such as having interactions with one new person each month. It may help to alleviate some pressure by including other colleagues whom you already know; this way, they can shoulder some of the conversation. Make the most of the interaction by making meaningful eye contact, being an effective listener, and sharing information.

3. *"As a woman, how could I be undermining my credibility without realizing it?"*

Here are a few of the most common ways. Do any apply to you?

- Do you speak very quietly and/or with upswing?

- Do you frequently defer to others—or allow people to interrupt you?

- Do you speak tentatively—or regularly preface statements with *"I'm not sure, but . . ."* or *"This may not be what you're looking for, but . . ."*

- Are you self-critical—or self-deprecating in front of others?

- Are you visually communicating confidence and professional-ism through your attire and body language?

- Do you over-apologize or get overly emotional?

- In meetings do you offer or default to be the notetaker?

- Do you pass on applying for promotions or leadership roles because you don't feel good enough?

- Do you deflect attention away from yourself to support others?

- Are you practicing perfectionism?

4. *"There is one person in particular with whom I want to build rapport. How do I ask someone to lunch or coffee when we've already been working together for a long time?"*

It's never too late to show gratitude or send a thank you note. The same concept applies to showing interest in building rapport with someone. Most likely, the person will respond positively—and feel important or flattered.

One approach is to acknowledge your commonality—and segue into an invitation that includes a specific time horizon:

> *"Darren, it occurred to me the other day that we've worked in the same office for a while now. It would be really nice to get together over lunch one day—or grab a coffee. Would you be up for it over the next few weeks?"*

There are many obvious advantages to being seen as credible and trustworthy. One specific benefit is that you are often given the benefit of the doubt or more of an opportunity to explain a mistake or fix damage to a relationship. Still, there are other times when no matter how trustworthy, credible, or hard you try—you fail. These important themes are addressed in the following pages. Join me for our final chapter as we explore the important aspects of recovering, rebuilding, and reestablishing.

CHAPTER SEVEN

RECOVERING, REBUILDING, AND REESTABLISHING

Failure is not a barrier to success, it's a stepping stone.
—ARIANNA HUFFINGTON
cofounder and past editor-in-chief of
The Huffington Post

Throughout your life's journey, there will be moments when you realize you have made a mistake, that an important relationship has been damaged, or that others' perceptions of you need to be changed. This is especially true if you're actively engaged in moving the dial of your success. In both your professional career and personal life, your mindset and actions will play a large role in how well you recover, rebuild, and reestablish.

THE ART OF FAILURE

There are many mindsets when it comes to failing. Some believe that failing is a critical component of success. It can lead to greater self-awareness, a heightened focus on important details, and impact us deeply enough for real change to occur. With failure comes learning. With learning comes increased understanding, which has the potential to propel you to a new opportunity because of these lessons learned. Leadership expert John C. Maxwell calls it "failing forward."

For me, failing is looking back and thinking, *"coulda," "shoulda," "woulda."* It's less about *not* succeeding at something and more about not even *attempting* it. For others, they may fear failing—because of the potential negative consequences to the relationships involved, the inability to meet the desired results, because it could be a hit to their reputations or self-esteem—which is understandable because sometimes mistakes are unfixable and unforgettable.

When I first started my career, I was hired for a keynote speech at a large global bank. The organizers didn't provide me with any guidance on what they wanted to achieve, and I didn't ask the right questions. As a result, my content missed the mark (this mistake turned out to be one of the unfixable ones). I learned valuable lessons—and when you can see how those lessons continue to positively influence present-day choices, it helps to heal the often negative feelings that surround the initial fail. Realizing that you don't need to completely forget the failure to be healed from it—and that both thoughts can coexist—can propel you forward. It's an important shift in mindset to think about failing as advancing self-growth and development.

In addition to learning from the mistake, how you handle the failure makes all the difference. Taking ownership is a very important aspect of demonstrating credibility and maintaining trust.

*The key is not that you failed; it's how you **handle** the failure.*

Culpability

Ownership can include apologizing, acknowledging, or being fully transparent with the reason behind the mistake. Examples of *not* showing accountability include making excuses, blaming others, minimizing the seriousness, or ignoring a mistake altogether. People are more apt to forgive when they like you, when they feel your intentions are true, sincere, and transparent, and when you show effort to try to rectify the situation. When taking ownership, there needs to be:

Humility over arrogance

Commitment over annoyance

Action over hesitation

Holding yourself accountable can mean the difference between losing credibility and being given the opportunity to recover.

Is it possible to recover from a mistake, rebuild rapport, and reestablish trust?
Yes.

Does it take a deeper level of self-awareness and an intentional effort on your part?
Absolutely.

Will it require open-mindedness and willingness from others?
Often.

Will it happen after one attempt?
Rarely.

Is success guaranteed?
No.

A Harvard University study showed that it takes approximately eight subsequent positive interactions to change someone's negative initial impression of you.[1] The thought of allocating that much time and effort can be daunting—especially when you're working, trying to schedule a lunch or coffee with friends, sneaking out early from work on a summer

Friday to see your child's sports game or recital, getting a few moments at the gym to relieve your daily stress, and trying to squeeze in a date night. Who has time to meet people eight times with the hope that they'll change their initial impressions of you? Still, this choice may not be ours to make. It takes time to show consistency of thought and action—and consistency is the key to recovering, rebuilding, and reestablishing.

The key is consistency of words, actions, and behaviors.

Consistency

Doing something once very rarely solidifies long-term results or a deep belief that things will be different. If you set out to shift perception through specific actions and behaviors, and you're not consistent in exhibiting those choices, you may never change that perception—and instead validate the one you're looking to replace.

Consistency leads to trustworthiness.

Trustworthiness inspires belief.

Belief allows the shift to happen.

Through consistent displays of positive behavior, thoughtful decisions, well-intentioned interactions, and smart choices you can help to rebuild trust and reflect your commitment to the desired outcome, thereby opening the door for the ideal change.

Howard Schultz, the founder and previous CEO of coffee giant Starbucks, has often referred to consistency as a "secret to success" with his over 30,000 stores across 78 countries.[2] When people know what they're getting, what they can rely on, what they can expect, they believe the experience, the interaction, and the choice they made will turn out positive. Belief is also needed to rebuild something that has been broken.

RECOVERING, REBUILDING, REESTABLISHING

Take a look at the following ten steps to start the process of recovering, rebuilding, and reestablishing:

- **Step 1: Assess your commitment.** Before you start on this journey, it's essential that you're committed to it. There has to be an authentic desire for change, void of any resentment, bitterness, anger, or blame accompanying your choice to change.

- **Step 2: Be realistic.** Think about how this situation came to be or what created the current perception. Take an honest look at what happened and what needs to shift.

- **Step 3: Increase self-awareness.** Do a deep dive into what *you* said or did to create this situation or have others form this perception of you. Others may have played a part; the focus must still remain on you.

  We can't control others' behaviors, actions, or choices; therefore, it's essential to put your energy into what you *can* control—what *you* could have said or done differently.

  What is *your* responsibility?

  How could your actions have been misinterpreted?

  What could have been another option to the one you chose?

  Now that you're self-aware of what went wrong and what you could have done differently, it's important to avoid falling into similar traps. Have a plan for how you will prevent the mistake or misperception from happening again.

- **Step 4: Practice.** Know what you want to say and practice saying it. Be sincere and use a moderate pace. Emphasize what will be different and what that person can expect going forward.

- **Step 5: Apologize, if required.** Is an apology required? If yes, follow the suggested Apology Template in Chapter 2 so that you reflect sincerity, professionalism, and accountability when having this conversation.

  If an apology has been given and it hasn't improved the situation, more effort may be needed on your part. Be kind to yourself as you keep on the journey of being open to how you can make things better.

- **Step 6: Take action.** The mistake that some people make is that they want to be forgiven by others, shift perception, or change a situation without actively replacing the old with the new. How can others start to perceive you differently if you haven't given them a reason to do so? How can you shift the wrong perception when you're not replacing it with a more accurate one? How can you expect others to forgive you when you have not practiced new actions that would start to heal the hurt? Words are just words and can be seen as hollow and meaningless if there are no actions behind them. Individuals want to know that you've given the situation thought, are going to act with intention to make it better, and will prevent it from happening again.

- **Step 7: Be visible.** You want to be visible showing the new behavior—if people don't see it, they don't know it exists. Find several opportunities to apply the new choices.

- **Step 8: Connect.** Engage individuals in your network to help you. Connect with key people in your workplace so that they're aware of what you're doing. Whoever the key players are in your inner circle, make sure that they also know what you're trying to accomplish. In tandem with your efforts, these individuals can help to shift others' perceptions of you.

- **Step 9: Tolerate the wait.** Give your decisions, behaviors, and interactions time to be realized and recognized. Be patient. Depending on the specific change you're working toward achieving, the personalities and emotions involved, and the degree of importance to the people who matter, you may not see results immediately. The longer the perception has been surrounding you, the more difficult it may be to change that perception.

The key is to align your expectations to the situation.

- **Step 10: Ask for feedback.** Once some time has passed and you've had a chance to consistently put your new choices into place, ask for feedback from people you trust.

    Do they see a change?

    What are they noticing that is different?

    Have others mentioned anything to them?

    Could perception be shifting, or does more work need to be done?

It's important to highlight a few points about feedback.

Asking for Feedback

Feedback can be empowering or unpleasant to hear. If you ask for feedback, be prepared to:

- Hear something you were not expecting

- Perhaps not be given any

- Listen sincerely to what's being said—without getting defensive or interrupting

- Have a prepared response—that reflects your appreciation, graciousness, and professionalism

If the person giving the feedback senses that you're offended or in disbelief, he or she may refrain from sharing future feedback. If you ask, be prepared for honest, straightforward input—listen. It can be a big indication of the respect this individual has for you when he or she takes the time—and potentially the risk—to share candid thoughts and honor your request for feedback.

The key is that with the ask needs to come appreciation.

Giving Feedback

- **Refer to the action as "feedback" rather than "constructive criticism."** When most people hear the term "constructive criticism," they unconsciously shut down or become defensive—because the word their brains center on is *criticism*. No one wants to sit there and be judged, which is often how people feel when they hear they're going to be given "good" and "bad" feedback.

- **Refer to the two types of feedback as:**

  - Developmental—if you want the person to modify or stop the behavior or action

  - Reinforcement—if you want the individual to continue the behavior or action

  The innate messages behind both terms are growth, development, and support, which are much more positive than the connotations associated with the word *criticism*.

- **Avoid the feedback sandwich.** When you say something positive—then negative—then positive, the recipient may subconsciously be waiting for the other shoe to drop. Any positive feedback will likely be overshadowed by the negative sentiments shared because the recipient may feel the positive's only being given to hedge the negative.

A more effective way of giving feedback is, throughout the project or year, to create a balance between developmental and reinforcement feedback and deliver it consistently. Find opportunities to authentically give reinforcement feedback. This establishes a more even playing field to share developmental feedback—and the receiver may be more receptive.

- **Be careful sharing unsolicited feedback.** Feedback is very personal. Therefore, an individual has to be in the right frame of mind to hear feedback—or he or she may feel blindsided by your words. Your good intentions can quickly turn to perceived judgment if developmental feedback is not properly presented. In addition, it's important to recognize when you're not in a position or don't have the established rapport to give feedback. If you give feedback without invitation, you may be irreversibly overstepping your bounds. If you're truly trying to help, ask if the recipient is open to, and would like to hear, what you want to share—and how the feedback shared could support his or her success.

QUICK TIPS

The Importance of Recognition and Feedback

Most professionals want to receive recognition and feedback. They want to know that their efforts are being acknowledged and appreciated—as well as if, and how well, they've met the expectations set. These two elements can be motivating, if given, and demotivating, if ignored. As a leader, it's important to find time to give performance evaluations or midyear reviews either formally in writing or more casually in a one-on-one meeting—even if it's not standard practice in your organization. How can someone be equipped, or inspired, to exceed expectations, max out their potential, or even commit to doing a good job if they don't feel valued or know what they could be doing differently to progress their success?

You've wholeheartedly completed all of the steps; you still may not be able to shed the previous perception, fix the damaged relationship, or improve the situation. What adds to the complexity of the situation is the personalities involved, the emotions felt, the frequency and duration of the occurrence, your likability factor, how trustworthy you are, the strength of the rapport, and the reputation you have built. It may take even more effort on your part to rectify the situation, or you may have to accept that a change will not come.

THE IMPORTANCE OF RESILIENCY

Sometimes you can't recover from a personal or professional choice or improve the current predicament. As you look back to understand what you could've done differently, you realize you made the decision with good intentions. You thought the decision was right at the time. You believed you had no other option.

For whatever reason, that choice didn't turn out well or the person is not forgiving you. If you find this to be the case, it's now time to focus on being resilient.

It's not easy to stay emotionally strong, be mentally tough, or avoid a defeatist mindset in the face of adversity, disappointment, or rejection. When life, relationships, and decisions don't go according to plan, it's time to focus on some key strategies, your inner strength, and people who can help get you through this difficult time.

The key is it's not how fast you bounce back;
it's how strong your effort is.

When it comes to practicing the art of resiliency, remember:

- **Breathe.** The breath reflects your state of mind—and how much of an internal toll the situation is taking on you. In order to overcome, you want to take back control of how much you allow this situation to affect you.

Emotional discomfort, angst, and anger need an outlet. Practice slow, deep breathing, meditation, or yoga and make time to go for a walk or exercise. The research is overwhelming as to the benefits of exercise on reducing stress, helping to relax the body, distracting and easing your mind, and calming the inner turmoil. It's incredibly important that in your quest to be resilient you now navigate from a mindset of strength.

- **Be kind.** If you've wholeheartedly tried to rectify the situation and have been unsuccessful, it's important to consider your own mental and emotional well-being. Sometimes no matter how hard you try, how sincere your apology, or how proper your actions, you're not given the chance by others to recover, rebuild, and reestablish. This is the moment when you need to be kind to yourself—and let it go. In this moment, remember that some of the most successful people also learned through failure . . .

> *You can only connect the dots looking backwards.*
> RAY DALIO
> Founder and Co-CEO of Bridgewater Associates, LP—
> the world's largest hedge fund

> *I did then what I knew best and when*
> *I knew better, I did better.*
> —MAYA ANGELOU
> American poet and civil rights activist

> *Sometimes you win, sometimes you learn.*
> —JASON MRAZ
> American singer songwriter, "I Won't Give Up"

> *We are only as good as the moment we're in.*
> *If we don't know better, how can we be better?*
> —LAURA JOAN KATEN
> Author of this book and supporter of your success!

COACHING CORNER

What do *you* say to soothe yourself after you've made an irreversible mistake?

- **Stay the course.** There's a chance that with time, your efforts will have an impact. There's no way of knowing how long it will take someone to heal. Don't give up. With care and consistency, stay the course of doing what you feel is needed to repair the situation or rebuild the rapport. You may find your patience pays off.

- **Start new.** If the old perception exists or the rapport is too damaged, it could end up stifling your success. You may want to change roles, departments, or companies so that you can start fresh and put your new practices into place.

Whether or not you were able to recover, rebuild, and reestablish, there will be a moment, an opportunity when you feel you can finally distance yourself enough from the situation to think about it without getting emotionally charged. This is an important moment of self-discovery, healing, and self-growth. Recognize this opportunity and think about what you've learned:

Are you more conscious now of what caused the initial issue—as you look back? Is there something you learned about yourself?

What would you do, or do differently, next time?

How will what you've just been through help you in the future?

Do you now have specific techniques for dealing more effectively with this type of person or situation should you face a similar scenario again?

Could your experience, and the knowledge gained, help someone else?

As painful, upsetting, confusing, or unfair as the occurrence may have been—look for something, no matter how small, that you can take away from the experience to progress your success, personal growth, or professional development.

The key is that your pain is not in vain.

When you have enough distance and feel you can truly look at the situation objectively, take a moment to step back and see what can be learned from the situation. With each lesson learned, you'll gain experience, wisdom, and self-compassion—and in the process create a strong foundation of communication habits to set you apart, help you leave a lasting impression, and support your continued growth.

Your Questions Answered

Common questions I am asked on the topic of recovering, rebuilding, and reestablishing include:

1. *"My boss has formed a misperception of me. What do I do?"*

    When at all possible, never leave a misperception lingering in the minds of others—especially when it comes to your boss. This person holds the power to support your success, and you don't want to be represented by the wrong reputation. Try the following techniques. Ask yourself:

    - What is the misperception that surrounds me?

    - What caused that misperception?

    - Are other people involved in fueling that misperception?

    - How long has the misperception been lingering?

- Have I done anything to support that misperception?

- Have I done anything to shift that misperception?

Sit down with your boss:

- After you answer the above questions, sit down with your boss. Make sure there's no miscommunication; you want to be very clear on what the misperception is and how it was caused.

- Communicate to him or her that you're actively working to rectify the misperception. When at all possible, share with your boss the actions you'll be taking.

- Ask for a follow-up meeting after you've had time to put those actions into place. You want to know if your boss is seeing a change, allowing for the change, and supporting your efforts— or if there's something else he or she needs you to do.

2. *"I'm very introverted, and I'm concerned it's holding me back. Without changing my personality, what can I do?"*

The following strategies can help:

- Bring a colleague along for new interactions to carry some of the conversation and act as a buffer.

- Try changing your hat. Think of it this way: When you put your "introvert hat" on, what characteristics are being represented? Perhaps being soft-spoken, enjoying conversations with one person versus many, working happily on projects alone versus in groups, or enjoying being the team player versus leading the project.

  Now put your "outgoing hat" on. For many introverts, it can be exhausting to try to be more outgoing. Therefore, focus on only one or two specific actions while wearing this hat, such as starting a conversation, speaking up first or second in the meeting, or volunteering to organize a department or team lunch.

- Be mindful of the balance. While wearing different hats, it's important that you make time to restore your spirit, center yourself, and recharge your batteries. If you're asking yourself to live outside of your comfort zone—and you do, well done. You also need to honor that you may need to "recover" from that experience.

3. *"What if I'm the one who doesn't want to let the other person recover?"*

The core focus of this chapter has been on what *you* can do to better your situation. Let's turn the tables and talk about what has been done *to* you.

You may have a very good reason for not wanting to mend fences with this individual—only you truly know. Self-awareness is sometimes the shortest distance to realizing whether or not a resolution is even possible from your perspective or if any solution could truly suffice. Therefore, here are a few questions for you to consider that may help you to take an objective look at the rationale behind your decision to stay your current course:

- *What is your biggest concern surrounding this situation or with this person?*

- *What core needs of yours are not being met by this person?* The need for respect, inclusion, safety, an apology, recognition, consistency of a more positive behavior, follow-through, trust?

- *Are there feelings of jealousy, envy, or resentment that are preventing you from looking at the situation rationally?*

- *Is not allowing this person to recover serving you well?*

- *Is he or she even aware that they have somehow alienated you?*

4. *"I find it very hard to forgive myself when I've made a mistake. Any advice?"*

Yes. First, know that you're not alone. We're often our harshest critic and most demanding customer. Also:

- The fact is that you're human—and with this comes an amazing capacity to learn. Sometimes you learn as you go, so we're bound to make mistakes along the way.

The key is that you learn from each mistake.

- Retrain your brain to be okay with less than perfection.

- Self-compassion is an extremely important part of your journey when it comes to recovering, rebuilding, and reestablishing— it's also very hard to be kind to oneself in the throes of a mistake. Honor your need to voice it or vent about it while also deciding to limit the time you live in this space.

- Focus on learning from your mistake and be proud when you've relied on that experience to prevent it from happening again.

FINAL THOUGHTS

We've come to the end of our journey together. This book was about progressing your success by giving you strategies to help you be more self-aware, informed, and empowered to take your success to the next level.

My goal was to first give you a clearer understanding of what contributes to other people's perceptions of you—and how *you* have the power to create an *accurate* first impression. Second, it was to share that key variables help to establish your credibility—projecting confidence and presence through your body, speaking with intention through your vocal delivery and words, and communicating your competence and value through your actions and interactions. In addition, if there's ever a hiccup in your journey, you're now equipped with techniques to recover, rebuild, and reestablish.

Every strategy highlighted in this book is focused on enhancing your strengths, eliminating undermining tendencies, and increasing your visibility. The information highlighted in this book can benefit you at any stage of your career, support your personal growth and relationships, and advance your professional development. (I continue to rely on these techniques in my own life.)

Use the information in this book as a guide as you make it your own. Above all else, be authentic by practicing only the strategies that you believe in. If not, they'll have the exact opposite effect because people will sense you're being insincere. It's important to always be aware of the reason behind your decision-making.

As you consider some of the shifts that you *do* want to make, the final question you may be thinking is, *How do I do all of this? It's awkward to start putting it into play. How do I start to tackle change?*

Here are your next steps . . .

NEXT STEPS

In any given moment we have two options:
to step forward into growth or step back into safety.
—ABRAHAM MASLOW
American psychologist

This is the moment. The moment when you decide how strong your commitment is to yourself. When you decide to start putting the techniques in this book into action, four things may happen:

1. Applying the techniques shared in this book will be a seamless transition.

2. Some techniques may take longer to feel natural and comfortable.

3. You may experience the "saboteur"—someone who, for whatever reason, wants to derail you and the courageous decision you've made to eliminate undermining habits and practice empowering techniques. He or she may say, *"You don't speak like that." "You've changed how you dress." "What's gotten into you? You're speaking so much in meetings now."*

    In that moment, you have a choice. You have an opportunity to reflect self-confidence, solidify your new path, and stifle any future questioning from this person by smiling and saying, *"Thanks for noticing."* Instantly you have reflected self-assurance and self-mastery. Or you can let this person's words dissuade you from the positive path you're on—and you can default to old behaviors.

    This moment will come. The choice will be yours. What is your level of commitment to progressing your success?

4. Many of the individuals with whom you interact will not know the information that you now do. You'll notice how many people undermine themselves or others. The question then becomes, will you role-model and share the information in this book? Sharing information is a whole other level of learning, leadership, sustaining rapport, solidifying credibility, and increasing visibility.

Throughout this book, I've asked you tough questions to increase your self-awareness and help you decide which actions to take and which changes to make. Now it's time to put your Action Plan into place.

ACTION PLAN

As you know, research reflects that when you write down your goals, you accomplish significantly more. *"People who very vividly describe or picture their goals are anywhere from 1.3 to 1.4 times more likely to successfully accomplish their goals."*[1]

Complete your Action Plan—so you can start seeing results. Thinking about the strategies in this book that resonated most with you, list one or two in each of the corresponding boxes.

Action Plan	
Put into place tomorrow morning	*Share with _____ within the next seven days*
Eliminate the undermining tendency of	*Biggest takeaway to remember*

NOTES

Chapter 1

1. Eric Wargo, "How Many Seconds to a First Impression?" Association for Psychological Science, July 2006, https://www.psychologicalscience.org/observer/how-many-seconds-to-a-first-impression.

2. Amy Cuddy, "First Impressions: The Science of Meeting People," Rob Capps Science, Wired, November 28, 2012, https://www.wired.com/2012/11/amy-cuddy-first-impressions/; "The Power of First Impressions Essay," http://www.123helpme.com/power-of-first impressions; and Shannon Polly, "First Impressions—the 7/11 Rule," Positive Business, October 27, 2015, http://positive businessdc.com/711-rule/ (article cites Michael Solomon, Marketing Department Graduate School of Business, NYU).

3. "Blue in Business," Empowered by Color, n.d., https://www.empower-yourself-with-color-psychology.com/blue-in-business.html.

4. "The Most Inspiring Coco Chanel Quotes to Live By," *Vogue* Australia, August 16, 2018.

5. Sylvia Ann Hewlett, Center for Talent Innovation Executive Presence, 2014.

6. Jason Beeson, "Deconstructing Executive Presence," *Harvard Business Review*, August 22, 2012, https://hbr.org/2012/08/de-constructing-executive-pres.

7. "The Soft Skills Disconnect," National Soft Skills Association, February 2015. These statistics were extrapolated from Charles Riborg Mann, "A Study of Engineering Education," published in 1918 by the Carnegie Foundation. The cited figures come from the data on pages 106–107.

8. 2018 National Association of Colleges and Employers survey.

9. 1980–2015, 83% increase in jobs requiring better interpersonal, communication, or management skills. Pew Research Center, The State American Jobs Report, 2016.

10. Tim Herrera, "Want to Seem More Likeable? Try This," *New York Times*, September 23, 2018, https://www.nytimes.com/2018/09/23/smarter-living/how-to-be-more-likeable.html.

11. Huma Khan, "Royal Etiquette: Do's and Don'ts When Meeting Her Majesty: Obama Sidesteps Traditional Gift Giving with a Fully Loaded iPod," April 1, 2009, https://abcnews.go.com/Politics/International/story?id=7228105&page=1.

Chapter 2

1. Sylvia Ann Hewlett, *Executive Presence*, Center for Talent Innovation, 2012, pp. 9–21.

2. Kunle Campbell, "Your Primer to the Psychology of Marketing: The Science of Emotional Buying and What Marketers Can Do About It," Ecommerce Marketing /How to Sell Online, BigCommerce, n.d., https://www.bigcommerce.com/blog /marketing-psychology/#how-to-speak-directly-to-emotions-the-limbic-system.
3. "Michelle Obama: 'When They Go Low, We Go High,'" CNN, July 25, 2016, https://www.youtube.com/watch?v=mu_hCThhzWU.
4. Christopher Wanjek, "Why Breathing Deeply Helps You Calm Down," Live Science, March 30, 2017, https://www.livescience.com/58480-why-breathing -deeply-helps-you-calm-down.html; and David DiSalvo, "How Breathing Calms Your Brain, and Other Science-Based Benefits of Controlled Breathing," *Forbes*, November 29, 2017, https://www.forbes.com/sites/daviddisalvo/2017/11/29 /how-breathing-calms-your-brain-and-other-science-based-benefits-of -controlled-breathing/#6a46f3de2221.
5. Kathryn Heath and Jill Flynn, "How Women Can Show Passion at Work Without Seeming "Emotional,'" *Harvard Business Review*, September 30, 2015, https:// hbr.org/2015/09/how-women-can-show-passion-at-work-without-seeming -emotional.
6. Founder of North Point Ministries, one of the largest Christian organizations in the nation. John Blake, "Two Preaching Giants and the 'Betrayal' That Tore Them Apart," CNN.com, updated November 2012.
7. Harris Eisenberg, "Humans Process Visual Data Better," Thermopylae Sciences + Technology September 15, 2014, http://www.t-sciences.com/news/humans -process-visual-data-better.
8. Marshall Rosenberg (October 6, 1934–February 7, 2015) was an American psychologist, mediator, author, and teacher. Starting in the early 1960s, he developed Nonviolent Communication, a process for supporting partnership and resolving conflict within people.
9. Dick Lee and Delmar Hatesohl, "Listening: Our Most Used Communications Skill," Extension University of Missouri, https://extension2.missouri.edu/cm150.

Chapter 3

1. CareerBuilder Annual List, January 9, 2014. Survey was conducted by Harris Interactive during November 2012 and included more than 2,600 hiring managers and 3,900 workers nationwide.
2. Amy Cuddy, TEDGLOBAL 2012, "Your Body Language May Shape Who You Are," TED video, 20:41, https://www.ted.com/talks/amy_cuddy_your_body _language_may_shape_who_you_are.
3. Valentine Zarya "How a Little Lipstick Could Add Thousands to Your Paycheck," *Fortune*, May 19, 2016, http://fortune.com/2016/05/19/makeup-more-money/ (covers the work of sociologists Jaclyn Wong of the University of Chicago and Andrew Penner of the University of California at Irvine); and Catherine Saint Louis, "Skin Deep: Up the Career Ladder, Lipstick in Hand," *New York Times*, October 2011, https://www.nytimes.com/2011/10/13/fashion/makeup-makes-women -appear-more-competent-study.html.

Chapter 4

1. Esther Snippe, "Your Speech Pace: Guide to Speeding and Slowing Down," SpeakerHub, January 19, 2017, https://speakerhub.com/skillcamp/your-speech-pace-guide-speeding-and-slowing-down.

2. Linda Geddes, "Why Do the British Say Sorry So Much?" BBC.com, February 24, 2016, http://www.bbc.com/future/story/20160223-why-do-the-british-say-sorry-so-much.

3. Anne Fisher, "Giving a Speech? Conquer the Five Minute Attention Span," *Fortune*, July 2013, http://fortune.com/2013/07/10/giving-a-speech-conquer-the-five-minute-attention-span/.

4. Reward Gateway, "The Top Three Demotivators of the Workplace: Lack of Recognition, Feeling Invisible or Undervalued, and Bad Managers," Cision PR Newswire, October 23, 2018, https://www.prnewswire.com/news-releases/the-top-three-demotivators-of-the-workplace-lack-of-recognition-feeling-invisible-or-undervalued-and-bad-managers-300735823.html.

Chapter 5

1. Mark Murphy, "Neuroscience Explains Why You Need to Write Down Your Goals If You Actually Want to Achieve Them, *Forbes*, April 15, 2018, https://www.forbes.com/sites/markmurphy/2018/04/15/neuroscience-explains-why-you-need-to-write-down-your-goals-if-you-actually-want-to-achieve-them/#462c99f47905.

2. Susan M. Heathfield, "How to Deal with a Bully at Work: Don't Allow Yourself to Become an Easy Target for a Bully," Human Resources Conflict Resolution, updated November 6, 2018, https://www.thebalancecareers.com/how-to-deal-with-a-bully-at-work-1917901.

Chapter 6

1. "What They're Saying," May 1977. The saying was ascribed to the creator of a successful U.S. supermarket chain called Bi-Lo; later attributed to Margaret Thatcher, former Prime Minister of England.

2. Alina Tugend, "Take a Vacation, for Your Health's Sake," International Business, *New York Times*, June 8, 2008.

Chapter 7

1. Kristi Hedges, The Do-Over: How to Correct a Bad First Impression," *Forbes*, February 10, 2015.

2. Martin Roll Business & Brand Leadership, "The Secret to Starbucks' Brand Success," Strategy, July 2017.

Final Thoughts

1. Mark Murphy, "Neuroscience Explains Why You Need to Write Down Your Goals If You Actually Want to Achieve Them," *Forbes*, April 15, 2018.

INDEX

A

Ability, 138, 199
  success and, 142
Accessories, 8–9
Accomplishments, 140, 193
Accountability, 109, 217
  partner for, 118, 200
Acknowledgment, 69, 108–110
  apologies and, 111
  interruptions and, 36–37
  response and, 134
  unresponsiveness and, 173
Action, 163, 220
  action plan, 233
  actionable statement, 57
  apologies and, 107
  behaviors and, 206–207
  credibility and, 199
  emotion and, 150
  time and, 106, 166–167
  validity and, 152
Active listening, 44–45
Admiration, 6
Affiliations, 207
Age, 160–161
Aggression, 32–36
Agreement, 50, 181
Alcohol, 20–21, 168
Ali, Muhammad, 61
Alignment, 2, 41
Angelou, Maya, 185, 225
Anger, 47
  aggression and, 32–36
  reactions and, 29–31
  tone and, 96

Answers, 194–195
Apologies, 220
  apology template, 105–111
  over-apologizing, 103–105
Appearance, 4–9
Appreciation, 38, 222
Arm crossing, 84
Arrogance, 25, 142
Articulation, 97–98
  impact and, 179–180
  of value, 196
Asking, 54, 183
  for feedback, 221–222
Aspirations, 7
Assertiveness, 34–35
  aggression and, 32–36
Assessment, 91
  of commitment, 219
  communication and, 185
  PACT and, 27
Attention, 31
  attention span, 33
  of audience, 89
  speakers and, 69–70
Attire, 5–8
Audience, 55, 89, 185
  credibility statement and,
    66
  distractions and, 78
  perceptions of, 40
  style of, 42
Authenticity, 187
Avoidance, 49, 105, 178
  of faux pas, 167–168
  opportunity and, 183

Avoidance *(cont'd)*
  paralleling and, 47
  professional anchor and, 77–78
  reading and, 56
  stances and, 80
Awareness, 168–169

B
Bad-mouthing, 50
Balance, 156
Behavior, 232
  action and, 206–207
  bullying and, 171
  character and, 202–203
  names and, 110
  pattern of, 149
  responsibility for, 104
Belief, 218
Benefits, 214
Beverage, 16
  alcohol, 20–21
Bloomberg, Michael, 185
BLOT. *See* Bottom line on top
Body language, 5, 175
  communication and, 85
  confidence and, 35
  focus on, 70
  impressions and, 71
  intensity and, 42
Body positioning, 82–83
Boss. *See* Leadership
Bottom line on top (BLOT), 53,
  189
Boundaries, 60
Bragging, 61
Brain, 26
  information and, 45, 63
Breathing, 30
  resiliency and, 224–225
  speaking and, 100
Buffett, Warren, 23
Bullies, 170–172
Business, 184

C
Calm, 166
Career, 40
Chanel, Gabrielle Bonheur "Coco," 8
Character, 198, 202–203
  competence and, 206–207
Characteristics, 33
  arrogance as, 25
  communication and, 5
Chitchatting, 178
  during presentation, 134–135
Choice, 83
  PACT and, 27
  patterns and, 149
  support and, 84
  word choice, 62, 89
Closing statements, 57, 65–66
Colleagues, 158
  saying no to, 156
Color, 5
Comfort, 14, 180
  comfort zone, 229
  relationship and, 159
  sitting and, 83
Commands, 31–32
Commitment, 153
  assessment of, 219
  consistency and, 199
  listening and, 47
Communication, 10, 90
  assertiveness and, 34–35
  assessment and, 185
  body language and, 85
  of character, 202
  characteristics and, 5
  communication styles, 33–34, 186–187
  competence and, 137–196
  confidence and, 90, 163
  in context, 125
  effectiveness of, 101
  face-to-face, 73
  hand gestures and, 75
  of message, 32

nonverbal communication, 86
 perception of, 91
 perspective on, 67
 respect and, 108
 of value, 143
 variation in, 173
Communication barriers, 126
Competence, 197
 character and, 206–207
 communication of, 137–196
 establishment of, 198–199
Compliments, 68
Composure, 26
 civility and, 169
Conciseness, 62
 language and, 189
 vagueness and, 52–55
Condolences, 110
Conduct, 10–11
Confidence, 20
 arrogance and, 25
 body language and, 35
 bullying and, 171
 communication and, 90, 163
 focus and, 85
 goals and, 124
 presence and, 71–87
Conflict, 174
Connection, 7, 220
 connectors and, 140
Consideration, 54–55
 conversations and, 174–176
 options for, 123
Consistency, 180, 199, 218
Context, 68, 125
Conversation, 38, 123, 146
 competence and, 137
 conversation zone, 76
 difficulties and, 174–184
 emotional conversations, 183–184
 empathetic listening and, 49
 escalation of, 192
 goals and, 163, 179

interruption and, 162–165
 monopolizer of, 39
 practice before, 177–182, 184
Conviction, 132
Corrections, 158–160
Courage, 162
Courtesy, 100, 177
 respect and, 134
Credibility, 55, 182
 credibility statement, 62–67
 establishment of, 197–214
 women and, 213–214
Cuddy, Amy, 71, 153
 power posing and, 80–81
Culpability, 216–218
Cultures, 103

D

Dalio, Ray, 225
Decisions, 145, 201
Deference, 193
Demands, 31–32
Devil's advocate, 151
Diaphragm, 100
Dichotomies, 145
Diplomacy
 diplomatic words, 126–132
 tact and, 127–131, 157–158, 173
Direct communicators, 154
Direct reports, 158
 saying no to, 156–157
Disagreement, 191–192
Discomfort, 195–196
Discretion, 121
Disrespect, 169–170
Diversion, 30
Doubt, 146, 209

E

Einstein, Albert, 52
Email, 133–134
 etiquette and, 210
 meetings and, 192–193
 prioritization and, 211

Emotion, 26
  action and, 150
  emotional conversations,
     183–184
  passion and, 39–42
  reaction from, 29
  speakers and, 46
  thoughts and, 148–149
  tone and, 96
Empathy, 110, 181
  apologies and, 111
  empathetic listening, 48–51
Employees, 120
Employers, 10
Empowerment, 174
Energy, 58, 79
  unfocused energy, 39–42
Engagement, 49, 76
  information and, 64–65
  presentations and, 135
  small talk and, 16–17
Enunciation, 98–99
Equality, 59
Etiquette, 209–210
  social business etiquette, 15–18
Evaluations, 3
Events, 15
Executive presence, 9, 26
Expectations, 221
Experience, 48, 229
  influence and, 144–145
Expiration date mentality, 105
Explanation, 161
Expression, 47
Extemporaneous structure, 57, 189
Eye contact, 73–74

F
Fabric, 5
Facebook, 60
Facial expressions, 73
  make-up and, 87
  nonverbal communication and, 86

Factors
  it factor, 31
  likability factor, 198
Facts, 65
Failure, 215–216
Faux pas
  avoidance of, 167–168
  handshakes and, 12–13
Fear, 152, 216
Feedback, 221–224
  eraser words and, 120
  praise and, 69
Finger shake, 12
Finger-pointing words, 125–126
Flat listening, 44
Focus, 58, 61, 70
  confidence and, 85
  results-focused style, 188
  on speakers, 43
Food, 16
Forward communication style,
  33–34
Friendships, 58–59

G
Gender, 40
Gesturing, 14
  hand gestures, 74–75
  nonverbal gestures, 126
  usage of, 76–77
Glove shake, 12
Goals, 65, 153
  alignment and, 41
  confidence and, 124
  conversation and, 163, 179
  mentor and, 7
  research and, 233
  tools as, 1
  for understanding, 231
Gossip, 102, 195–196
Graciousness, 142
Gravitas, 26, 176–177
Greenberg, Alan ("Ace"), 186

Greetings
  alternate greetings, 13–14
  credibility statement and,
    63, 66
Grooming, 9
Guidance, 7, 140
Guidelines, 139

H

Habits, 23
  self-monitoring of, 133
  uptalk as, 93
Hand gestures, 74–75
Hands, 75
  open hands, 78–79
Handshakes, 11–13, 18–19
Harvard Business Review, 9, 40
Harvard University, 217
Hearing, 42–43
Honesty, 140
Huffington, Arianna, 215
Human resources, 170
  bullying and, 171
Humility, 141–142
Humor, 102
  diffusion with, 162, 196
  response to, 160–161
Hygiene, 9

I

Idea, 132
  influence and, 212–213
  support and, 41
Impact, 189, 226
  articulation and, 179–180
  impact statement, 182
Imposter syndrome, 146
Impressions, 23–70
  body language and, 71
  perceptions and, 1–21
  research on, 3
  stimuli and, 3–4
Indirect communicators, 154–155

Inflection, 96–97
Influence
  communication and, 90
  experience and, 144–145
  idea and, 212–213
Information, 2, 63, 231
  complexity of, 94
  correction of, 158–160
  engagement and, 64–65
  listening and, 42, 53
  references to, 55
  resource and, 166
  sharing of, 67–68
  transmission and research, 45
Initiative, 33
Insecurities, 208
Intelligence, 141
Intention
  disrespect and, 169–170
  speaking with, 89–135
Interactions, 10–11
  equality and, 59
  etiquette and, 15, 210
  limits on, 169
  passion and, 40
Interjection
  interruption and, 36–37
  template for, 37–39
Interruption, 150
  conversation and, 162–165
  interjection and, 36–37
  leadership and, 164–165
Introverts, 213
  concerns of, 228–229
Invisible backpack, 144–146
Invitations, 143

J

Jargon, 102
  over usage of, 124
Jefferson, Thomas, 53
*Journal of Personality and Social
  Psychology*, 17

K

Kindness, 145
  mistakes and, 162
  resiliency and, 225
Knowledge
  knowledge-share, 144
  rapport and, 204–205

L

Language, 46, 102, 172. *See also* Body
    language
  competence and, 137
  of leadership, 189–191
  nonverbal language, 79
  speaking someone's, 185–191
  value and, 46
Leadership, 159
  interruptions and, 164–165
  language of, 189–191
  listening and, 43
  misperceptions and, 227–228
  praise and, 120
  rapport and, 59
  saying no to, 155–156
Learning curve, 208
Letters of recommendation, 139
Likability quotient, 31
Lincoln, Abraham, 137
LinkedIn, 60
Listening, 32, 55
  discretion and, 121
  hearing and, 42–43
  levels of, 44–51
  listening gap, 52
  studies on, 51
Location, 175–176

M

Make-up, 87
Mantra, 81–82
Maslow, Abraham, 232
Maxwell, John C., 216
Meetings, 15

checking in at, 159
email and, 192–193
lateness to, 108–109
misperceptions and, 86
Memorization, 56
Mentor, 7, 139
  work/life balance and, 200
Message, 115–116, 164
  communication of, 32
  nonverbal messaging, 45
  open hand as, 78–79
  softening of, 34
Mindset, 81
  failure and, 216
  shift in, 148–152, 200
Misperceptions, 86, 131
  leadership and, 227–228
  tone and, 101
Mistakes, 230
  kindness and, 162
  ownership of, 109–110
Monotone, 97
Motivation, 140
Movement, 84–86
Mraz, Jason, 225

N

Names, 19
  behaviors and, 110
  credibility statement and, 63
Negotiation, 193
  compensation package, 194
Networks, 203
  cultivation of, 205
New York Times, 87, 201
Nin, Anaïs, 1
Nodding, 50
Nonverbal communication, 79
  facial expressions and, 86
Nye, William Sanford, 141

O

Obama, Michelle, 28
Observations, 178–179

Opportunity, 39, 194
  avoidance and, 183
  demands of, 208
  salary and, 195
  self-discovery and, 226
  smiling and, 87
Options
  for consideration, 123
  imprint and, 190–191
Outcome, 56, 149
  solution and, 190
Outlaw, Frank, 197
Overcompensation, 209
Ownership, 217

P

Pacing, 93–94, 95
PACT. *See* Pause, assess, choose, take
Paralleling, 46
Participation, 21
Parties, 15
Passion, 39–42
Passive listening, 44
Pat shake, 13
Patterns, 6, 149
Pause, 27
  active pause, 118
  vocal delivery and, 95
Pause, assess, choose, take (PACT), 27–28
Pens, 78
Perceptions, 72, 85. *See also*
    Misperceptions
  of affiliations, 207
  of audience, 40
  of communication, 91
  impressions and, 1–21
  subjectivity of, 18
  words and, 2
Personal space, 12
  protection of, 14
Personalization
  apologies and, 106
  email and, 210

Perspective, 152
  on communication, 67
  wall of, 30
Pitch, 92–93
Positivity, 195
Posture, 79, 177
  Power posing and, 80–81
Power-play shake, 13
Practice, 41, 153
  before conversation, 177–182, 184
  skills and, 43
  tongue twisters, 98
Praise, 68–69
  leadership and, 120
Presence, 9, 26
  confidence and, 71–87
Presentation, 74
  chitchatting during, 134–135
  of content, 42
Prevention, 106–107
  self-awareness and, 219
Prioritization, 190
  email and, 211
Professional anchor, 77–78
Professional development, 138
Professionalism, 141, 164
  apologies and, 108
  self-awareness and, 16
  social media and, 60
Progress, 123, 227
Projects, 143
Pronunciation, 99
Protocol, 19
Proximity, 83

Q

Qualifications, 139

R

Rapport, 58
  apologies and, 107
  to build and sustain, 204–205
  commonality and, 87, 204

Rapport *(cont'd)*
feedback and, 223
introverts and, 213
leadership and, 59
trust and, 198
Reaction
anger and, 29–31
response and, 25–27
Reading, 55–56
Recognition, 109
of dichotomies, 145
employees and, 120
feedback and, 223
Recording, 169
speaking and, 98
Rectification, 106
References, 55–56
Reflective listening, 45–48
Relationships, 54, 159
rapport and, 204
relationship-centered style, 188
Repeat offenders, 181–182
Reputation, 54
solidification of, 164
Research, 17
on exercise, 225
gender and, 40
goals and, 233
gravitas and, 26
on impressions, 3
on information transmission, 45
stress-relievers, 201
visualization and, 146
Resiliency, 224–227
Resource, 166
Respect, 23, 122
communication and, 108
courtesy and, 134
Response, 155
acknowledgment and, 134
blindside and, 28–29
email and, 211
to humor, 160–161

to praise, 68–69
reaction *vs.*, 25–27
unresponsiveness, 172–173
Responsibility, 104
Results, 54
results-focused style, 188
Reward Gateway company, 120
Role, 64, 160
Roosevelt, Franklin Delano, 53, 189
Rosenberg, Marshall, 48

S
Salary, 193–195
Sarig, 104
Saying no, 154
to direct reports, 156–157
to leadership, 155–156
Schultz, Howard, 218
Seat choice/placement, 83
Self-awareness, 132, 229
increase of, 219
professionalism and, 16
self and, 24
undermining and, 4
Self-compassion, 227, 230
Self-discovery, 226
Self-doubt, 146
Self-inventory, 29
Self-promotion, 61, 138
self-sabotage and, 143–144
Self-sabotage, 138, 232
self-promotion and, 143–144
self-sabotaging words, 121–124
Self-talk, 147–148, 200
Sharing, 57, 166
information, 67–68
observations or concerns, 178–179
Silence, 50
Simplicity, 62
Sitting, 82–84
Situations, 153
personalities and, 224
removal from, 172

Skills, 10, 43
Small talk, 20
   engagement and, 16–17
Smiling, 74, 86–87
Social media, 60
Solution, 190
Sorry, 104. *See also*
   Apologies
Speakers, 43
   attention and, 69–70
   emotion and, 46
   engagement and, 49
   pace for, 94
   respect and, 122
Speaking, 98
   with intention, 89–135
Standing, 80
   speaking and, 100
Stanley, Andy, 43
Statements, 49, 57
   credibility statement, 62–67
   impact statement, 182
   transition statement, 37–38
   WIIFT, 65
Stiffness, 80
Stimuli, 3–4
Strengths, 138
Stress-relievers, 201
Students, 139
Studies, 120, 217
   on appearance, 9
   on conduct, 10–11
   on listening, 51
   on make-up, 87
Style, 6, 42
   communication styles, 33–34,
      186–187
   flex of, 187–189
Subjectivity, 18
Success, 67, 142, 231
   conduct and, 10–11
   humility and, 141
   small talk and, 20

Suggestions, 194
Support, 41, 172
   choice and, 84
   transparency and, 208
Sympathy, 48

T

Tact, 127–131, 157–158, 173
Technology, 77
Terminology, 58–59
Thoughts, 38, 147
   adjustment of, 151
   emotion and, 148–149
Time, 56, 210
   action and, 106, 166–167
   consistency and, 218
   conversation and, 176
   lack of, 25–26
   to process, 30
   time tone, 135
Title, 64
Tolerance, 168–169
Tone, 96, 176
   misperceptions and, 101
   time tone, 135
Tools, 1
Transparency, 208
Trust, 197
   consistency and, 218
   rapport and, 198
Twain, Mark, 89

U

Uncertainty, 188
Undermining, 212
   self-awareness and, 4
   undermining words, 102–103
Understanding, 46, 124
   empathy and, 181
   goals for, 231
Uptalk, 34, 90
   vocal delivery and, 93
Urgency, 123

V

Vagueness, 52–55
Validity, 151–152
Value, 63, 138
  articulation of, 196
  communication of, 143
  of guidance, 140
  language and, 46
Verbal presence. *See* Vocal visibility
Visibility, 165, 220
  credibility and, 205
  vocal visibility, 92
Visualization, 146
Visuals, 76
Vocal delivery, 89, 112, 177
  communication and, 91
  pace and, 93–94, 95
  pausing during, 95
  pitch and, 92–93
  tone and, 96
  volume and, 99–101
Vocal variety, 96–97
Vocal visibility, 92
Voice, 35–36, 175
  as instrument, 97
  pitch and, 92
Volume, 99–101
Volunteering, 144

W

WBTI. *See* Workplace Bullying and
  Trauma Institute

What's in it for them (WIIFT), 62
  leadership and, 189
  statement about, 65
Winfrey, Oprah, 186
Women
  credibility and, 213–214
  handshakes and, 18–19
  make-up and, 87
Woolf, Virginia, 212
Words, 2, 47, 167
  actions and, 220
  attributes and, 24
  charged words, 124–126
  diplomatic words, 126–132
  eraser words, 51, 119–120
  filler words, 115–119, 133
  mispronunciation of, 103
  name association with, 19
  self-sabotaging words, 121–124
  undermining words, 102–103
  usage of "and," 120–121
  weak words, 111–115
  word choice, 62, 89
  words per minute, 94
Work/life balance, 200–202, 209
Workplace, 137, 175
  bullies in, 170–172
  situations in, 153
Workplace Bullying and Trauma
  Institute (WBTI), 171

ABOUT THE AUTHOR

 **Laura Joan Katen** travels over 100 days a year for speaking engagements. She divides her time by giving keynote talks at various national conferences, leading group training programs, and facilitating one-on-one coaching sessions on the topic of Communication for clients across the United States and Canada.

Laura is the author of the strategies book *How to Communicate with Confidence, Clarity, and Credibility*. She is president of KATEN CONSULTING, a New York–based *certified* 100 percent women-owned professional development training company. KATEN CONSULTING conducts group training programs and one-on-one coaching sessions in four key topics: Executive Presence, Communication Skills, Individual and Team Presentations, and Business Social Etiquette.

Laura works as an adjunct professor in the Communications Department at Manhattanville College in Purchase, New York; is a Business and Dining Etiquette specialist, having attended the Protocol School of Washington; received her Bachelor of Fine Arts degree with extensive training in Voice and Speech from Carnegie Mellon University; and simultaneously attended Chatham College to study Education. Prior to cofounding KATEN CONSULTING in 2003, Laura began her corporate career in the financial services industry at Merrill Lynch.

Laura can be found online at www.katenconsulting.com, @katen consulting, and www.linkedin.com/in/katenconsulting.